1939
1945

50 years ago on Sunday, 3rd September 1939 to be exact, many children in Britain wondered why their parents looked worried as they sat listening intently to the voice of Mr. Neville Chamberlain, the Prime Minister on their wireless sets. The gentleman was busy informing the nation that they were now at war with Germany. Poor old Neville seemed genuinely upset to have to relay this piece of unpleasant information and his audience were no doubt equally upset to receive it.

The announcement of war probably had little effect on the majority of children. They still ran outside to play as usual but the changes to their young lives would come soon enough.

Factories disappeared beneath gallons of camouflage paint, shop windows were patterned with sticky tape, sandbags appeared in huge piles around important buildings, people everywhere started to wear uniforms and floating in the air above the rooftops like giant silver-grey whales were the barrage balloons.

Posters on walls carried slogans like, 'GROW YOUR OWN FOOD,' 'DIG FOR VICTORY,' 'SAVE FOR DEFENCE,' 'MAKE-DO AND MEND,' 'BE LIKE DAD – KEEP MUM!,' 'CARELESS TALK COSTS LIVES' and 'IS YOUR JOURNEY REALLY NECESSARY?'

At home, the windows were blacked out and the garden was dug up to make way for an air raid shelter. Finally the bombs came raining down bringing death, destruction and a severe alteration to the landscape on a daily basis.

Children were evacuated to unfamiliar places, had to wear gas masks, sleep in air raid shelters, collect salvage, have their supply of sweets severely rationed, wear clothes that followed the 'make-do and mend' order, say goodbye (sometimes forever) to fathers and older brothers and suffer neglect due to the long working hours imposed on their parents by the war.

Through all of this, there remained one institution that still catered exclusively for children and although it suffered from paper rationing, its main aim was to entertain and bring a smile to the faces of its readers. The kid's weekly (or fortnightly) comic.

The comic strips offered a liberal dose of morale-boosting humour and just a hint of propaganda in their full colour, two colour or plain black and white cartoon panels. Many of these cheap and cheerful little publications disappeared in the blitz or into the ravenous jaws of the paper salvage drive but a few survived and were even cared for by collectors so that today we have the chance to inspect them again and get a fascinating glimpse of a little corner of the war that has been largely overlooked.

Now read on . . .

Other books about Comics by Denis Gifford

Discovering Comics
Stap Me! The British Newspaper Strip
Victorian Comics
The Great Cartoon Stars
Happy Days: One Hundred Years of Comics
The British Comic Catalogue
British Comics and Story Paper Price Guide
The International Book of Comics
The Complete Catalogue of British Comics and Price Guide
The Encyclopaedia of Comic Characters
British Animated Films

Text and compilation Copyright © 1988 by Denis Gifford

Acknowledgements
All the comics reproduced in this book come from the author's personal collection. The comics are copyright of the original publishers, D.C. Thomson and Co. Ltd., of Dundee, and Fleetway Publications and IPC Juveniles, inheritors of the old Amalgamated Press titles. Grateful acknowledgement is made to the publishers, and particularly to the original artists, writers and editors who unfailingly brought laughter to children at a time closer to tears.

Cover Art & Interior Design by MIKE HIGGS GRAPHICS

ISBN 0 948248 85 8

Published by
HAWK BOOKS LTD.,
Suite 411, 76 Shoe Lane,
London EC4A 3JB.

Copyright © 1988 Hawk Books Ltd.

Printed in Portugal

Conditions of Sale: This book is sold subject to the condition that it shall not, by way of Trade or otherwise, be lent, re-sold, hired out, or otherwise circulated without the publisher's prior consent in any form of binding or cover other than that in which it is published and without a similar condition including this condition being imposed on the subsequent purchaser.

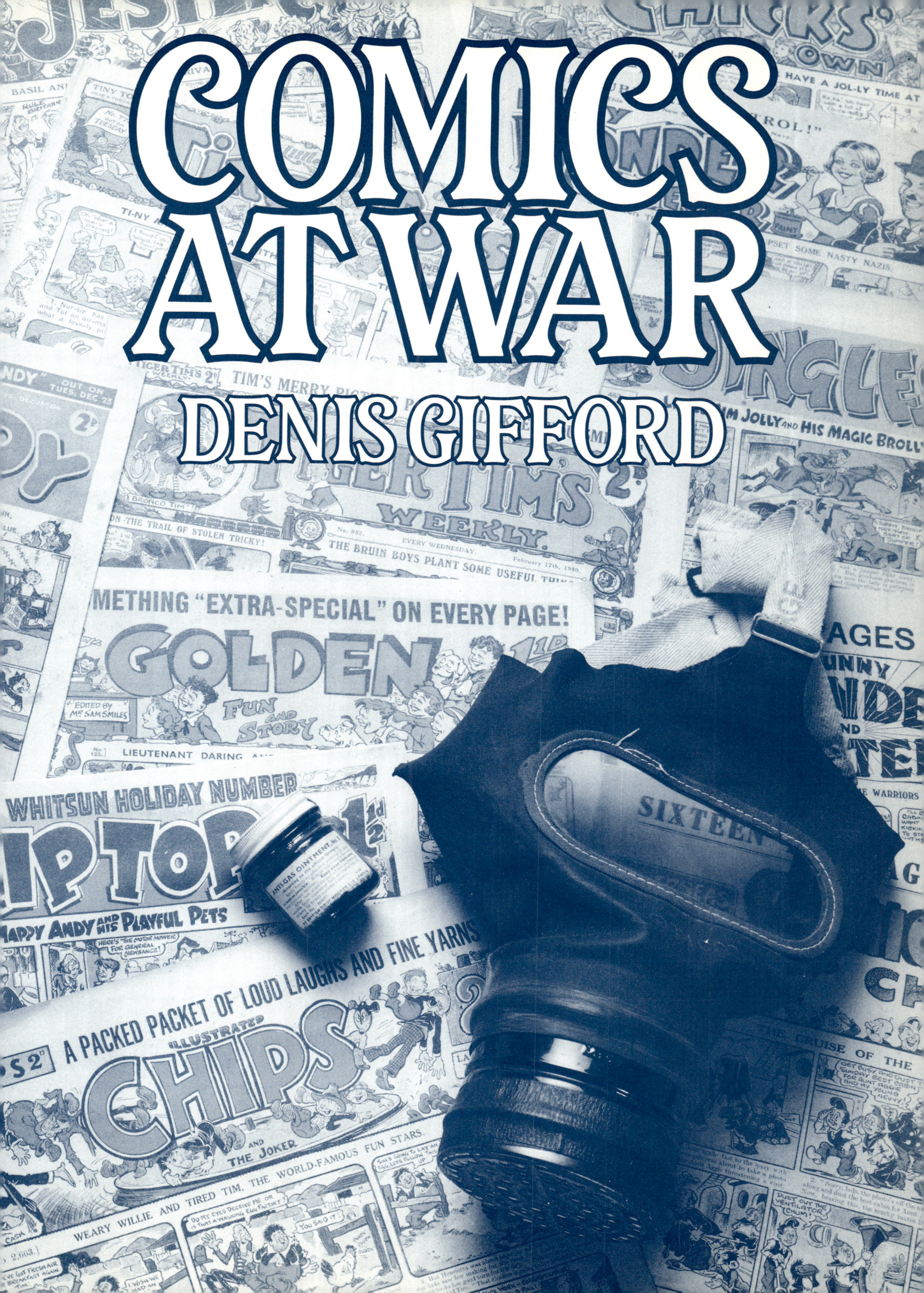

ALL THE FUN OF THE WAR!

Or, How Basil and Bert Boffed Old Nasty's Noggin!

The day war broke out was not, as Robb Wilton and other eminent historians claim, September the third, 1939. It arrived with a cry of "Heil me!" on October 21st, and I have the document to prove it. This piece of paper is pink, cost one penny, and is entitled **The Jester,** number 1,980 to be precise. And eye-witnesses to this event were none other than Basil and Bert, Our Very Private Detectives. (Their surnames were obviously Top Secret).

The shape of things to come, a shadow no bigger than a geezer's beezer, had been cast in this comic as early as November 19th, 1938. Basil, he of the monocled peeper, and Bert, his scruff-topped sidekick, had been accidentally incarcerated (and you know how painful that can be!) in the dank dark depths of Dunjun Isle. The bewhiskered old bathbun sharing their cell turned out to be none other than H.R.H. King Tinpantz, ruler of Rubberdubbia. In a trice, or, as there were but two of them, a twice, B. and B. had the whiskery one squatted on his rightful throne and his dirty deposer dumped in the drink. And thus did British Justice deal a swift uppercut and two veg to Dick Tater the Dictator.

"I'm King of ze Castle once more!" cried Kingy, "You must take zis enormous reward, and blow ze National Debt!" Basil and Bert accepted the sack marked 'Ninepence' with greedy graciousness, and one week later were off on the trail of new adventures, glory, and soss-and-mash.

And thus we see that even publications as humble as children's comic papers had their Munich. Dick Tater the Dictator came and went from the front page of **The Jester** within a week or two, but just like his real life counterpart, a dictator with the even funnier name of Schickelgruber, he was only off-stage in the wings, biding his time for a comeback.

It happened in the first week in January of that fateful year of 1939. Basil and Bert were on a mission to locate Miss Luvly's lost treasure, which had turned out to be an oversize diamond. Then the trail took a twist into something more sinister. The gem, or 'jool' as we know it in the comics trade, took on all the attributes of an Alfred Hitchcock 'MacGuffin'. It was revealed to be the long-lost Eye of the Sacred Billiken. Naturally it was nabbed from Miss Luvly's hot little clutch before you could say Jack Robinson, (or Jakey Rubinstein if you were Issy Bonn), and B. and B. were off in yet another trice, plus Puss-Puss plane. If was all aboard for Taterland, where a hole in the heel of your striped sock was the proud badge of the Storm-taters, and where Dick Tater the Dictator ruled with cries of "Three hails and a couple of yodels!", and issued proclamations reading "Everyvun vatch everyvun else, cos novun's to be trusted vun inch! Hail me!"

Our Very Private detectives were up to their red, white and blue eyeballs in dark doings in Taterland. It was the adventure of a lifetime, if not a laughtime, and for the first time in the hitherto happy history of children's comics, cognisance was being cogged of the way the grownup world was wagging.

Let Tiger Tim and the Bruin Boys bedevil benign Mrs Bruin with their wayward wheezes, or Happy Harry and Sister Sue belabour Poor Old Pa with their pesky pranks. Chucklesome foolery was fine for **Rainbow** and **Crackers** and the double dozen other comics that brightened my boyhood in 1939. But such was not for Mr A.G.B. Parlett, comic artist extraordinary, who drew the front page frolics of Basil and Bert for **The Jester.** He plunged his halfwitted heroes into a potty parallel of another kind of front page, those of dad's daily newspapers which our comics came wrapped in.

And Mr Parlett poked his jokes at those grownup papers, too. A passenger in the Puss-Puss plane to Taterland is buried beak-deep in his copy of **The Daily Dumps.** The headlines read 'Outlook Black' and 'Situation Grim', and if you borrow Basil's monocle you can just make out the back page racing results: '1 – Blue Hump; 2 – The Pip; 3 – Jitterbug.' Just a little sideline smile showing us the worries of the real world of January 14th, 1939. Stand up who said children's comics don't reflect life!

Then, with a cry of "Don't make a hole in the clouds, it makes the sky look as if the moths have got at it!", Basil and Bert are parachuting into Taterland on the trail of Herr Pin and the Sacred Billiken. But despite all the dashing Fraulein Pretty can do to help, which isn't much as her Uncle is the dreaded Dick Tater himself, our lads find themselves in the Dickory Dock on trial by Joory: 'Twelve good Taters with no specs!' Taterland prisoners are guaranteed a fair trial. Note the notice: 'No dark specs allowed in ze Jury!'

The Prosecuting Tater makes his speech. "Hail Tater! Do you find zem guilty or not innocent? Ze evidence says zey are, and it's good evidence, even if I says it as I wrote it!" With a chorus of Hail Taters ze Joory gives its verdict. "Ve find zem guilty, and please may ve go home to dinner!" Clapped into Prizzing Kamp, our daresome duo are given a choice of lunch: onion soup, onion soup, onion soup, or onion soup. They chose onion soup. "Knock it back while its wet!" advises the warder. The boys promptly do as advised, knocking it back through a barred window and all over D. Tater himself! "That'll bring tears to your eyes!" laugh the lads, thus keeping the jolly old flag a-flying. The Onion Jack, no doubt.

Complications and spuds fly thick and fast. In the Bank Holiday Bumper Number of June the third, Basil and Bert, wrecked aboard the Good Chip Flying Spud, are fished from the drink by none other than the Prime Minister, the Rt Hon Neville Chamberlain himself, doing his best to hide under the alias of Charlie Chilblain. The P.M. is on his hols, using his pet umbergamp as a fishing-rod to teach worms to swim.

July finds Baz and Bert fielding for the Stormtaters Cricket Club (Rules: Dick Tater is Never Out!). August arrives and the boys depart for England, Home and Kippers – 1,975 miles as the Flutterby Flits – driving Dick Tater's brand-new second-hand Rollsalong 40-Tater-Power Superspud. "After we escape we'll put treacle in the tank and post it back to him," promises Basil. But woe is us and them. Within weeks a chance meeting with a mortar mixer turns the 'tecs into solid statues, something of a shock for Herr Tater when he unveils them in mistake for Flupstein's Statchoos of Adam and Madam!

When September and the real war arrived, all seemed lost. The Right Orrible D. Tater, S.P.U.D., was galloping up his path to Bloatersgarden, jool in mitt, chuckling "I vant to be alone, like Garbo! If she vos here, ve could be alone togezzer!" Once again the Billiken beamed, wearing his umpteen-carat eyeball. "Hail!" hailed D.T., "Nobody can use your empty eye-socket as an ashtray again!" But the foolish foreigner reckoned without British brawn, the downfall of many a station sandwich!

"Pounce on the old tater, sir!" cried Bert, "Show him we mean peace, even if we have to spifflicate him to get to it!" Basil pounced. "Hold that, Tater!" he hooted, landing a fast fist on the no-good's neck. "This is where you get it on the place you always forget to wash!" Old Tater was well and truly stung: he ended up on a bed of nettles. And Dick Tater was never seen again!

'Cos why? 'Cos that happened on October 14th, 1939. Next week's issue was dated October 21st and **The Jester** was at war. The time lag from September the third was, of course, the seven week's stockpile, a necessary interim between real time and publication time to allow for writing and drawing and editing and block-making and printing and distributing the comics to the corner shops.

And thus it was that we children of England, fed up and far from home, evacuees all, came face-to-fizzog with War's Grim Reality seven weeks later than the long-trousered lot who read grown-up comics like the **Daily Mirror**. For here in **The Jester**, in black-and-white (sorry – pink!), was the truth for all to see.

Basil and Bert looked the same as ever, their usual half-witted selves. But who was this goose-stepping through the pictures? This was no Dick Tater heavily symbolised with a sossidge-nose and a walrus-moustache in case Herr Hitler sent the **Jester** Editor a sharp note from his solicitor. This was the real thing, 'Ateful Adolf 'imself, complete with flopping forelock and toothbrush tash. Gone was the Stormtater symbol of the heel-holed sock, replaced by the Crooked Cross of the Sinister Swastika. The Nasty Party had arrived, holding its first meeting (in the Ricebag, of course) to 'decide who to diddle next.' Adolf came first with a fistful of promises, "to be busted ven it suits me, so vot!", to be followed in close order by General Snoring, Dr Gobbles and Herr Von Drippentop.

This, at last, was the signal, the comics' call to arms. Fire Over England, or at any rate, over Fleetway House, Farringdon Street, where the comics came from. Inside the **Jester,** Constable Cuddlecook swapped his blue helmet for a tin titfer and went on blackout beat. Over at **Comic Cuts,** Big Hearted Martha Our Clever Cleaner heard the call to arms, rolled up her sleeves, and became Big Hearted Martha Our A.R.P. Nut: peanut – get it? The Crusoe Kids clobbered Admiral Von Hamburger's pocket battleship, Der Ditchland, with a flying sossidge, while Plum and Duff, the Boys of the Bold Brigade, walloped Old Nazty and Fatty Boring, carting them clinkwards with a carol of 'Roll Out the Barrel.' And in **Chips,** Laurie and Trailer Our Secret Service Lads enlisted in the Coldcream Guards when their arch-enemies, Crown Prince Oddsocksz and Serge Pantz, suddenly shifted accents from red Russki to something more Jerry-built.

Soon Scotland came in on our side as the Dundee **Dandy** and **Beano** went into battle. When Addy and Hermy the Nasty Nazis arrived in the pages of **Dandy,** and Musso the Wop (He's a Big-a-da Flop) turned up in **Beano,** war in the comics had clearly come to stay. For the duration, at any rate. For seven long years Britain's comics kept her youngsters laughing, despite all that Hitler & Co – and an ever-decreasing paper ration – could do. This book forms a long overdue tribute to the artists and writers, editors and publishers, who Did Their Bit in an all too easily forgotten field that is Forever England.

Denis Gifford
Sydenham 1988

No. 1,941. BASIL AND BERT, OUR VERY PRIVATE DETECTIVES. January 21, 1939.

1. Basil and Bert have come down in the world in more ways than one. They were after Herr Pinn, Dick Tater's spy, who had Miss Luvly's diamond. Bert couldn't get his parachute to work.

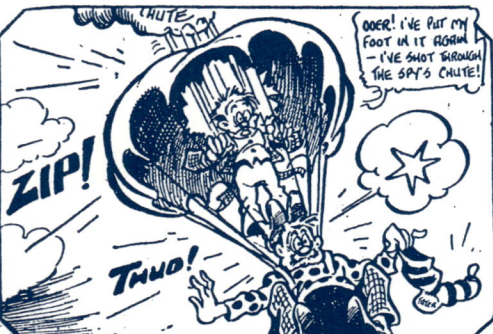

2. "Pull the rip-cord on your parachute," cried Basil. But he was too late. Bert had put his foot in it, or rather gone right through Pinn's parachute and given him a tap.

3. "Good for you, Bert," the posh detective yelled, raising his hat like the perfect gentleman he always is. "I'm glad to see you've come to earth at last, old lad."

4. Bert did come to earth right on top of Herr Pinn, and with a bump that made his false teeth rattle so much the frontier guardsmen thought a machine gun was firing!

5. Dick Tater himself was a big man with big corns and big ideas. He used the wart on the back of his neck for a collar-stud. Dick Tater had just heard about the stolen diamond.

6. Dick Tater rung the hooter for his Stormtaters, who were sitting in the mess-room making a mess of the place, throwing orange peel and peanut shells all over the floor.

7. "No longer will Taterland be a one-eyed joint," said Tater, "for Herr Pinn is returning with the diamond for ze one-eyed billiken. Call out all ze brass bands and lay hot dogs for two in ze dining-room," he added with a growl.

8. Herr Pinn didn't seem to like his scent-sheller being scraped along the ground by Basil and Bert in their search for the diamond. It suddenly fell out.

9. No doubt most of you have heard about the gold rush. Basil and Bert did a diamond rush, for the "sparkler" started rolling down the road.

10. Herr Bunn, the leader of the welcome party, was really leading the band up the garden, as it were, because Herr Pinn, the spy, had lost the valuable diamond, and Basil and Bert thought that they were going to lose it as well.

11. The two deflectives—sorry, detectives—properly upset things when they barged into the welcome party. Bert didn't notice the commotion for the diamond was his.

12. "Now let's go and have a cup of coffee," Bert said, as they ambled towards a cafe. "We got the diamond back without any trouble!"

Basil and Bert; Jester; November 1939; (George Parlett); © Amalgamated Press

THE JESTER 1D. EVERY SATURDAY.

Aeroplanes Given Away! See Page 7.

JESTER 1D.

No. 1,983. **BASIL AND BERT, OUR VERY PRIVATE DETECTIVES.** NOVEMBER 11, 1939.

1. Basil and Bert, the private detectives, were in Dictatorland doing a spot of Secret Service work (Hush, hush!). They spotted 'Ateful Adolf, the Nasty Dictator, painting the town red.

2. "Don't take any notice of the old Nasty!" laughed Basil, striking a match on Adolf's back pocket. 'Ateful Adolf flared up properly when he heard this.

3. Adolf didn't like people striking matches on him and he rose to the occasion. He picked up his pot of paint made from imitation tea-leaves and poured it on Basil and Bert, making Basil lose his match.

4. As Basil's match burnt through the rope, the Nasty dictator came off his perch and did a nosedive into a barrel. "Behold! The mighty are fallen," muttered our monocled one, his features plastered all over with paint.

5. General Snoring was showing off his nice new uniform to Dr. Gobbles and Herr von Drippingtop. "Nice, ain't it?" he chuckled, speaking in broken or, rather, cracked English.

6. By this time, the paint was beginning to obscure our 'tecs' vision. Running round a corner, they ran right into the fat general!

7. General Snoring nearly had a couple of pink fits with blue trimmings when he saw the paint on his uniform. Basil and Bert decided to do a bunk!

8. "Help! The enemy are advancing!" yelled Bert, his teeth rattling like a load of peanuts. "He who fights and runs away lives to fight another day. Quick, hide in that dustbin, Bas!"

9. Bert played follow-my-leader and followed his old school-chum into the dustbin. In the barrel near by, 'Ateful Adolf was coming up for the third time when Bert put the tin lid on him!

10. 'Ateful Adolf was in a proper temper! Ooh, he was cross! He started to leap about trying to escape from the barrel, and old Snoring thought it was our 'tecs. "Grab 'em!" he cried.

11. "We will drop de interfering 'tecs into der river!" snarled Snoring, lifting the barrel up. 'Ateful Adolf tried to tell who he was but they wouldn't believe him!

12. Snoring, Gobbles, and Drippingtop hurled their leader into the wet. The next tick they caught sight of our 'tecs and they nearly had a couple of pink fits with yellow trimmings.

(You must see what happens to the 'tecs in Taterland next week! Have you told your friends about these remarkable pictures?)

7

THE PAPER TO BRIGHTEN THE BLACK-OUT!

You'll never feel blue with this pink comic!

THE JESTER 1D. EVERY SATURDAY.

No. 1,984. — BASIL AND BERT, OUR VERY PRIVATE DETECTIVES. — NOVEMBER 18, 1939.

1. Basil and Bert, the famous detectives, were in Dictatorland doing a spot of Secret Service work. They suddenly spotted 'Ateful Adolf and General Snoring.

2. "Quick! Hide!" whispered Basil. "Here comes the Nasty Dictator!" The prize detectives dodged into a near-by tailor's shop and made a noise like moths.

3. "Look at this lovely bit of cloth," said General Snoring, picking up Basil's coat. "I'll cut a piece off and use it for patching." He pulled out an overgrown penknife and gave a swipe.

4. "Oi! You leave my coat-tails alone!" yelled our monocled 'tec, dodging neatly aside. Old Snoring was so surprised, his sword chopped a chair in half. "Three chairs, I mean, cheers!" cackled Bas, leaping away.

5. "'Tis Baseel!" yelled the Nasty Dictator. "After him, Hermann!" Bert was standing near by disguised as a dummy. "Don't point, Adolf!" he murmured. "It's bad manners!"

6. "I like zat sound almost as much as I like myself," grinned 'Ateful Adolf, as Bert gave Snoring a hearty thump with his boot.

7. General Snoring thought it was Adolf that had dusted his boots on his trousers. "Funny, isn't it?" he grated. "I'll learn you! Gr-r-r!"

8. "I'll dust your ear for you now," continued Snoring, giving Adolf a clout on the listener. Basil was coming to earth in quite a hurry.

9. Basil came down with a rush and Snoring got it properly in the neck. "Help! Landslide!" he cried as the rolls of cloth rolled down.

10. When Dr. Gobbles looked in he saw the two Nasty leaders in a dead faint. "What's all this?" he said.

11. "There now, take a rest!" said Gobbles, plonking Hermann gently on a chair. But the chair happened to be the one Snoring had cut in half, and it collapsed on Adolf. "Grhx! Himmelgerblitzen!" screamed Adolf.

12. Snoring was too dazed to take any interest in the proceedings, so the old Nasty gave Hermann a large bite. "'Ateful Adolf looks rather hungry!" cackled Bert.

13. "Old Adolf isn't hungry, he's angry!" laughed Basil. "The public will fall for me when I tell them how I made the Nasties fall!"

(More big laughs with the detectives in Dictatorland next Saturday! These are the pictures that are giving Hitler indigestion!)

JESTER 1d

THE JESTER 1d. EVERY SATURDAY.

GARY COOPER In "THE SIOUX TRAIL!" See Page 8.

No. 1,985.   **BASIL AND BERT, OUR VERY PRIVATE DETECTIVES.**   NOVEMBER 25, 1939.

1. Basil and Bert, the detectives, were on secret service in Nastyland, so keep quiet about it, won't you! Our 'tecs weren't keeping quiet themselves, however, singing "Rule, Britannia!"

2. When our detective-lads reached the line: "Britannia rules the waves!" 'Ateful Adolf leaned out of the window and gave them another wave—a wave of soapy water.

3. After a while, Basil and Bert began to sit up and take notice and the first thing they noticed were a whole lot of notices pasted on the wall. They were Nasty orders.

4. Our detectives didn't care two hoots for all the Nasty orders in the world and they painted saucy remarks over the notices. "What a sauce!" cried Herr Gobbles and Herr von Drippingtop.

5. Those two high-placed Nasties made remarks in low German, with cries of "Heil Adolf!" and "Attaboy!" they launched themselves to the attack.

6. Herr Gobbles and Drippingtop descended upon our 'tecs like a sack of kitchen-nuts, and pressed our coconibs' faces in the dust. Then they caught sight of the saucy remarks and laughed.

7. Meanwhile, in the Reichstag, 'Ateful Adolf was having a plate of seig-"fried" sausages and Reich-pudding (no relation to good old English rice-pudding). 'Ateful Adolf snarled.

8. The sounds of Nasty laughter floated through the window and old Adolf never did like laughter—it gave him a pain in the waistcoat. Lashing out with a spoon, he knocked General Snoring's medals flying.

9. Those medals certainly put Herr Gobbles and Drippingtop on their mettle. Yelling like ants with earache they pelted down the street.

10. "Your face looks 'paint'-ful!" cried Basil, seeing the paint on Bert's features. "Let me wipe it off or they'll take you for a Red Indian!"

11. Basil mistook Adolf's tablecloth for a piece of old rag, and as he gave it a tug, the Nasty leaders din-din went sailing through the window right into our 'tecs' arms.

12. Our detectives had the German sausages naturalised by sticking a Union Jack in them! Then they toddled off with their booty and everything looked "bootiful"—until Adolf's face appeared at the window!

BE PREPARED!
(TERRIBLE TERRIERS AND MERRY MILITIAMEN!)

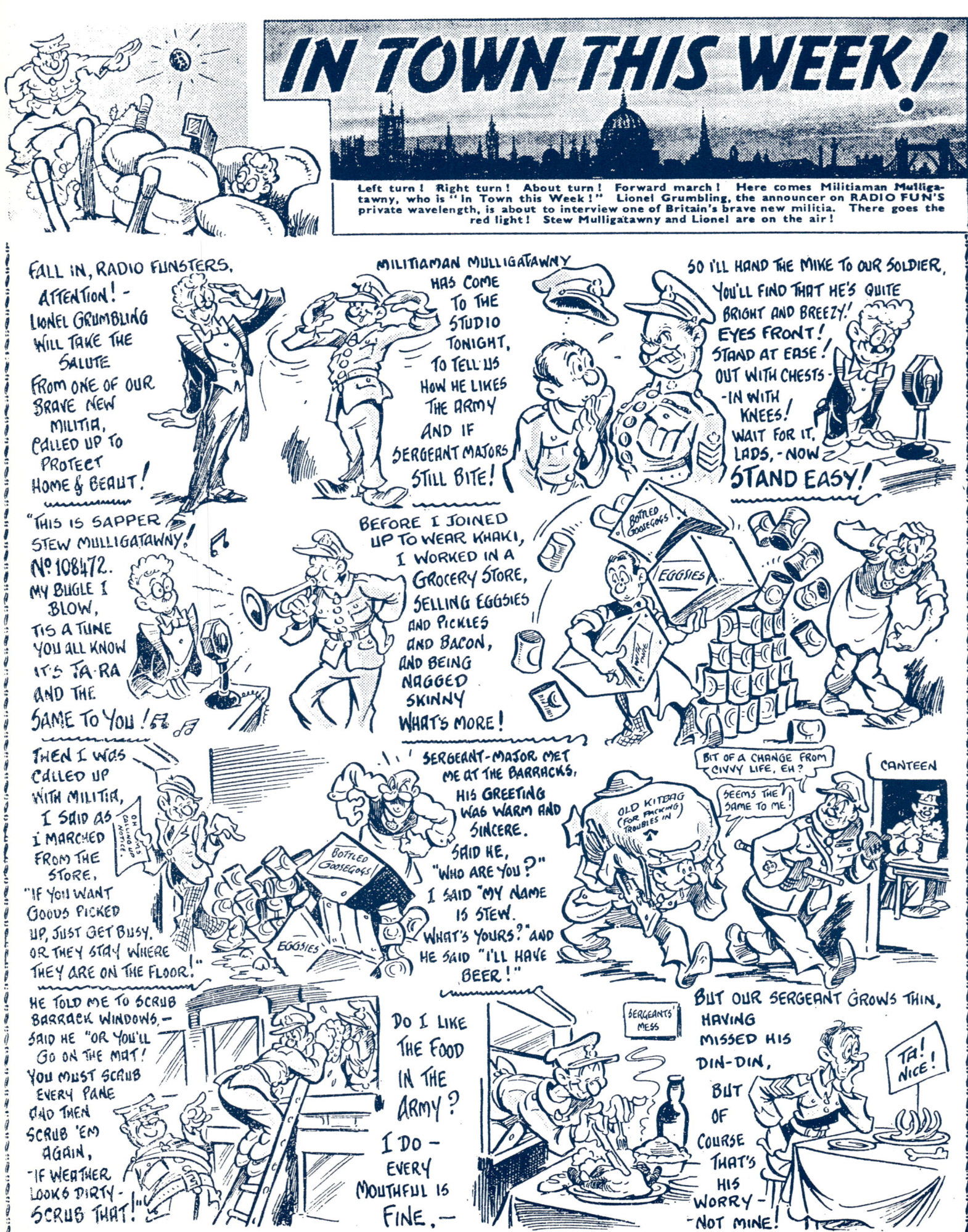

Even in the piping days of peace there was a slight touch of the old khaki and blanco about British comics, hanging about from the Great War of 1914-1918. A brace of bright Boy Soldiers called Plum and Duff, billed as 'The Boys of the Bold Brigade', put the weekly wind up Sergeant Suet and Colonel Bogey in peace, war and peace, signing on in **Comic Cuts** in 1926, serving right through the Second World War, and finally being pensioned off in the final issue of their comic, on 5 September 1953, not a day older or an inch taller for all their record 27-year service. We shall meet them in action against Adolf later. Meanwhile in May 1939, the Territorial Army was busy recruiting a sparetime soldiery. So were the comics. Marmaduke the Merry Militiaman joined the stars in **Radio Fun,** and Sandy and Muddy, 'The Two Terrors of the Terriers,' clocked on in **Knockout.**

In Town This Week; Radio Fun; August 1939; (George Parlett); © Amalgamated Press

SANDY AND MUDDY --- THE TWO TERRORS OF THE TERRIERS.

Sandy and Muddy; Knock-Out; August 1939; (Norman Ward); © Amalgamated Press

MARMADUKE, THE MERRY MILITIAMAN.

Marmaduke The Militiaman; Radio Fun; August 1939; (John Jukes); © Amalgamated Press

AT WAR WITH THE ARMY

Once war had been declared and Prime Minister Neville Chamberlain had unfurled his umbergamp, the comic call-up began in earnest. Characters fell over themselves and each other in their rush to enlist, not always with success. Simon the Simple Sleuth, Hugh McNeill's weedy weakling, was passed A1, but by an M.O. who turned out to be Old Nasty in disguise, seeking to weaken our army! Weary Willie and Tired Tim, 'The World Famous Tramps' from **Chips**, had bonked the Boers in the Nineties, and Kyboshed the Kaiser in 1914, but failed to foul-up der Führer this time. But as cockeyed cookhouse-wallahs their potatoes had appeal. Other comic stars lent a hand from the civvy sidelines: Desperate Dan's whiskers made useful bayonets while Deed-a-Day Danny, another McNeill winner, did his boy scout's best.

KOKO the PUP

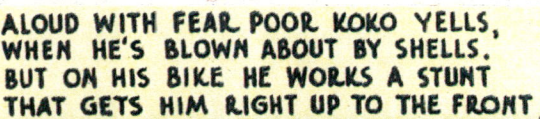

ALOUD WITH FEAR POOR KOKO YELLS, WHEN HE'S BLOWN ABOUT BY SHELLS. BUT ON HIS BIKE HE WORKS A STUNT THAT GETS HIM RIGHT UP TO THE FRONT!

Koko the Pup; Magic; July 1940; (Bob MacGillivray); © D.C. Thomson.

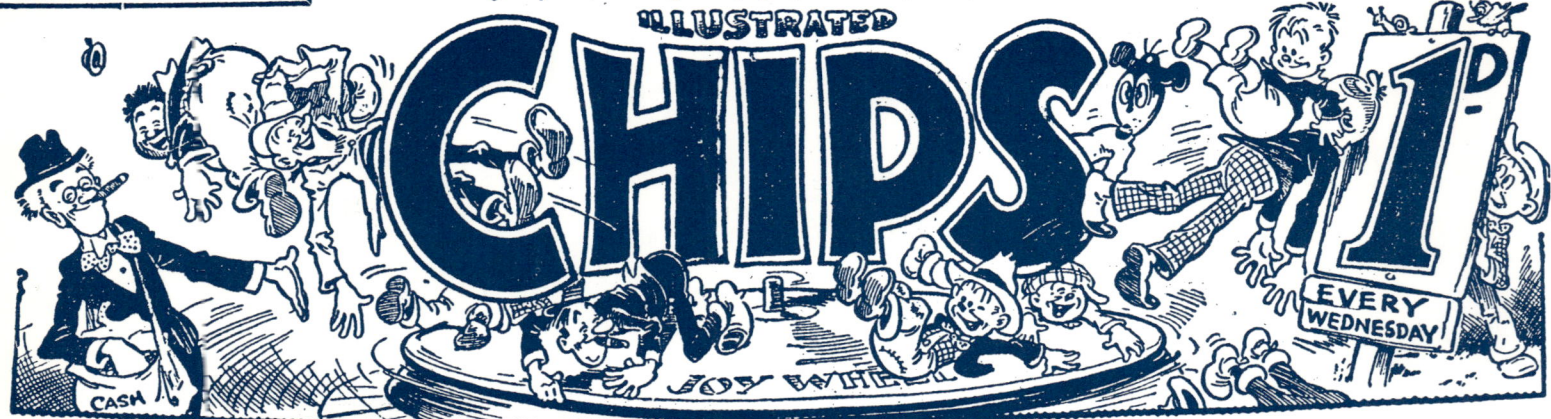

WEARY WILLIE AND TIRED TIM, THE WORLD-FAMOUS FUN STARS.

[No. 2,583.] [March 9, 1940.]

1. Dear Chipites.—Standing one day at an army cookhouse door Willie and Tim spotted a cookhouse wallah coming out with his pay. "Corks, there's money in this," gulped Willie.

2. A few ticks later they cast their peepers upon the enticing notice which you see above. "Cooluvadumpling," parped Willie. "Twenty pounds a day for removing spuds' overcoats!"

3. So being a bit short of twenty pounds a day, they applied for the job and got it. "You'll do," said the sergeant cookie. "I'll see you get twenty pounds each, straight away."

4. And so they did, a double dose of twenty pounds of spuds. Then they rumbled that they had made a mistake about the notice, and that it meant weight and not wealth. Dear-dear.

5. But having signed on the dotted line, they had to get on with the job. "Crumbs, this peeling lark doesn't ap-peel to me," moaned Tim. "I've never been in such a scrape before." And the sight was enough to bring tears to the spuds' eyes.

6. Then, as if Tim hadn't got trouble enough already, he got an eyeful of the juice of an onion, which had got in among the veg's by mistake. "Coolummy," gurgled the tubby one. "This is enough to put a chap off his onion, it is!"

7. And that onion juice gave him a bad attack of weeps in the peepers, just as two very stylish A.T.S.'s appeared on the scene. And they thought that he was wallowing in weeps, because he was thinking of home sweet home and his dear mum.

8. So they promptly adopted old Tim and carted him off to the canteen for cakes and comforts. "Sob no more, little man," they soothed. "We'll be a couple of mothers to you." And wasn't Willie jolly well wild about this? You bet he was!

9. "I'll have to try a basinful of this sob stuff," he fluted, so he prepared to throw a dummy in the canteen doorway. "Every time I think of my old dad's face I want to faint!" he bleated. "I've got one coming on now. I want to faint."

10. "Then have it on us," said a couple of ambulance chaps, who were handy on the scene. "Swing a swoon on our little carrier." "Ooer!" moaned Willie. "Bring me plenty of nourishing buns and a gargle of pop before I go right off!"

11. But he went right off, all right, 'cos the well-trained first aiders carried him off. "Poor old Willie's come over a bit coperzootic, I'm afraid," purred Tim. "I hope those kind-hearted gents will give my playmate a drop of something."

12. They did give him a drop, too, because he fell clean through the stretcher, and he has never felt so down-trodden in all his puff. It's no fun to get a faceful of foot, but you can't help laughing, can you? Though William did not smile.

13. But he got his comforts after all, though he wasn't exactly in the mood to enjoy them. And I don't suppose that Tim's guffaws of mirth did him much good, either, but he'll be all right again for next week's fun.—Thine, Corny Chips.

Desperate Dan; Dandy; March 1940; (Dudley Watkins); © D.C. Thomson.

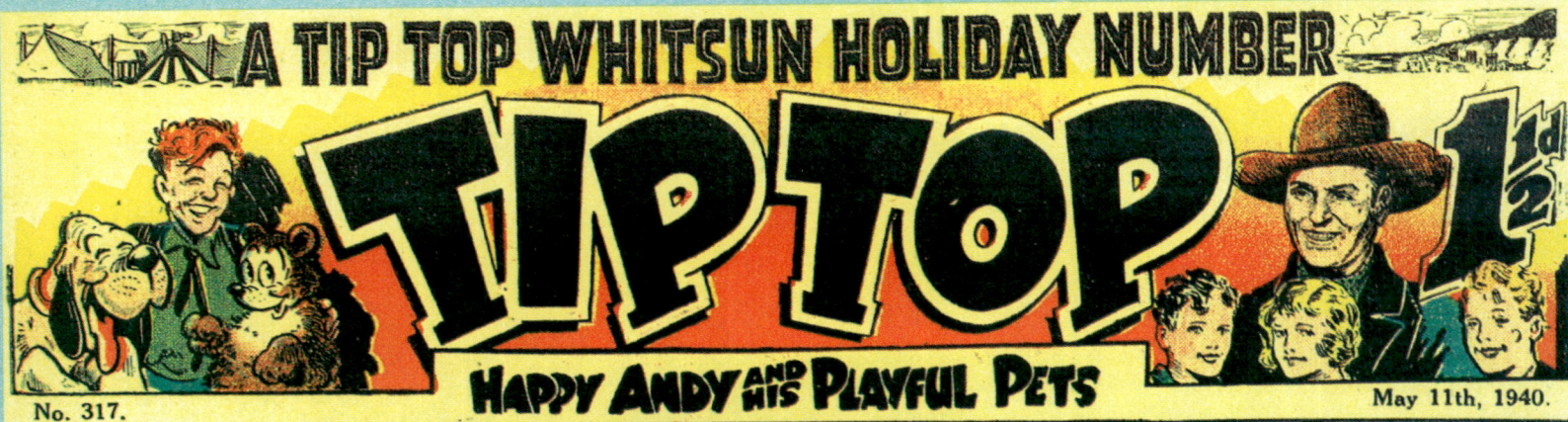

No. 317. *May 11th, 1940.*

1. A few days before Whitsun the manager of Harker's Store sent for Andy and said that General Newsance had ordered a new motor-mower for his garden. "You can deliver it," said the manager. "But mind how you go. Don't exceed the speed limit, my boy!"

2. Well, Andy drove carefully and reached the general's house without mishap. His pets went, too, and while our little lad introduced himself to the maid, Sugar and Candy inspected the mower. "This is a funny machine," murmured Candy. "Do you think it's a kind of steam-roller or a one-horse-power motor car?" "I've no idea," grinned Sugar. "Perhaps it's a machine for slicing bacon or cutting the whiskers off a goosegog. It's a marvellous machine."

3. The pets were truly carried away by the mower, but in more senses than one! By accident Candy pressed the starting lever and that started a packet of trouble. "Wow! We're being taken for a ride!" gasped the pets.

4. But it was hardly a ride! It was like a nightmare, though much more unpleasant. The pets were certainly put through it for the mower charged through a brick wall into a lily pond. "It's our bath-night!" cried Sugar.

5. There was no stopping the mower. It raced on, wrecking a rustic arch and then crashing into a dove-cote. Everything in its path was smashed completely, and if a steam-roller had been in the garden the mower would probably have tried to go through that, too!

6. "Wow! This is more exciting than a ride on a switchback," gurgled Sugar. "You're right," agreed Candy. "It's worse than trying to ride a frisky camel with the toothache. I'll certainly get the 'hump' if this mower doesn't stop soon." The mower didn't stop.

7. There's a saying that walls have ears and if this is true the walls of the summer-house must have got the ear-ache for the mower shot through the place like a knife going through a piece of butter. The pets *were* "upset."

8. Even more upset was Happy Andy who felt very *unhappy* at this moment. "This is the last straw," he gasped. "The garden looks like a rubbish dump after a cyclone. I shall get the sack through all this."

9. Soon General Newsance turned up and his moustache turned up in surprise when he saw the damage. "Boy!" he roared. "Did your motor-mower do all this?" "Y-y-y-es," gulped our chum. "Shall I patch up the wreckage, General?" "No, of course not," snapped the old soldier. "Everything in the garden is lovely. It couldn't be better!"

10. "Order me lots of mowers," he said. "The 'mower' the better. Then I will smash my way through the jolly old Siegfried Line and take Berlin or bust." How Andy and the pets grinned at all this.

(*Next week Andy and his pets have a funny adventure with a model railway at the store. Order your TIP TOP to-day.*)

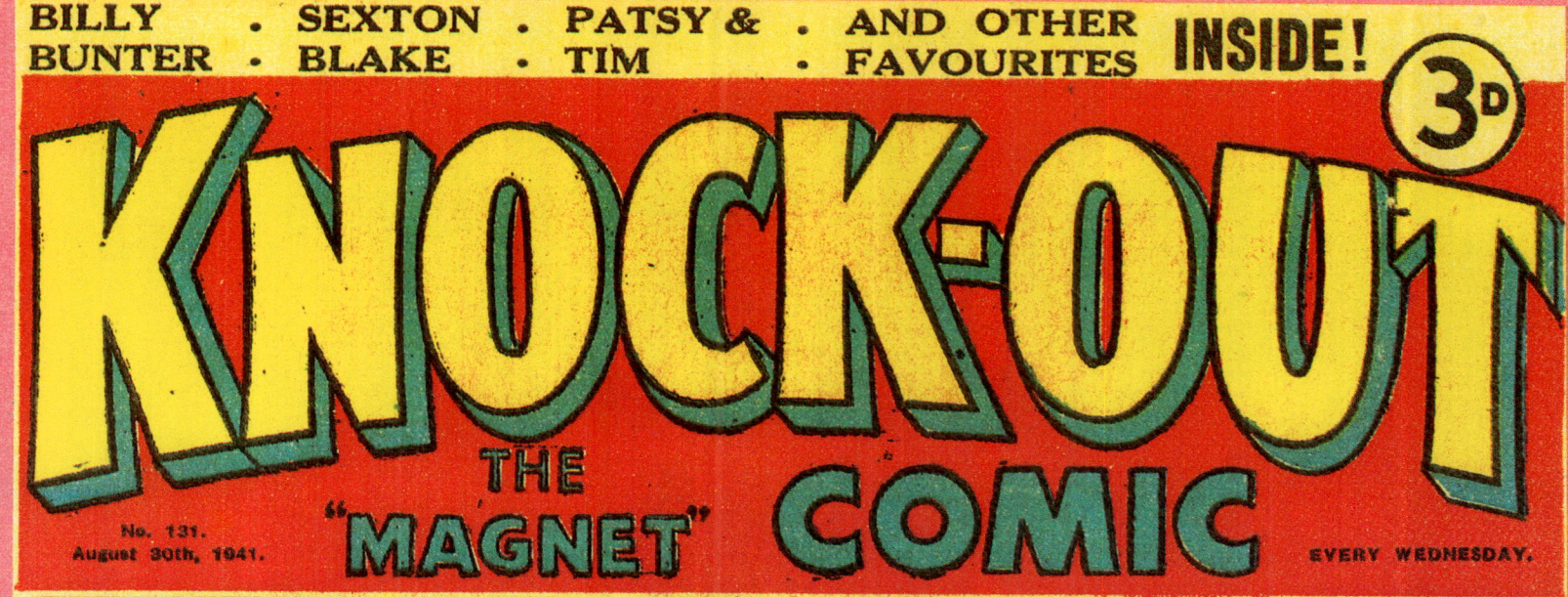

OUR ERNIE
MRS. ENTWHISTLE'S LITTLE LAD.

Cried Colonel Blanko, "Hi! my lad—
You're just the fellow I want, by gad!
You take this letter to Italy—
It's for my brother, and urgent—see?"

Now Colonel said our lad must go
By shortest route there were, and so
On map lad drew a line from home
Across the Alps, and down to Rome.

Then, leaping on to iron steed,
Off he shot at terrific speed.
Ploughing his way o'er moor and fen,
Through dale, up hill and down again.

He bounced his way to cliffs of Dover,
Shoved peg on nose, and then went over,
Landed in Channel with splosh and swish,
Scaring shrimps and scattering fish.

Then up and over Atlantic wall.
And though our lad were very small,
The Nasti's started up a blitz
With notion of blowing lad to bitz.

A river bridge he crossed were mined,
But enemy were all behind.
So only reward for Nasti sappers,
Were loads of bricks upon their nappers.

Next thing lad struck were railway track,
And on same line but farther back,
Were hefty armoured train, which had
A gun trained on our lickle lad.

And out of gun a shell came whizzing,
Which caught up lad, then started fizzing,
As though it knew that Ernie E.
Were on his way to the 8th Armee.

Cried Charlie, "Ee, what can we do?
We're in the soup, lad—and the stew!"
But just then tunnel came in view
Which saved the day, and Ernie, too.

On, on he rode, through shot and shell,
Flame-chuckers, mortars, bombs, as well;
Through battle lines, in midst of strife,
At risk of limb, and also life.

Until, at last our gallant kid
Caught up with Colonel's bruvver Sid,
Who'd just knocked off to have his tea
And so, for half an hour, were free.

So Major Blanco read the note
His bruvver, Colonel Blanko wrote:
It were, wiv luv from Alf, to say,
What would he like for his birfday?

Our Ernie; Knock-Out; February 1944; (A.J. Kelly); © Amalgamated Press.

UNCLE DAN
THE MAGIC MAN

At the army barracks one fine day
Dan hears a real tough sergeant say,
"Come on, you loafer." With a smack
He hits that poor young private's back.

Dan sees the Colonel coming now,
And so he waves his magic bough
Right o'er him. Gosh! Oh gee, by gum!
A tramp that Colonel has become!

That sergeant don't like tramps about,
And straightway with an angry shout,
He lands the "tramp" a mighty kick—
Once more Dan waves his magic stick.

The sergeant don't half get a scare
To see the Colonel standing there.
He doesn't quite know where to look
As he's called every kind of crook.

In the mess-room Danny hears the men
Say that their dinner's late again,
But that rotten sarge has got his food
Dan waves his wand—this will be good!

Now all the men laugh at that rotter,
For his food has changed to bread and water.
He waves his arms and stamps his feet,
But—no! He can't bring back his meat!

His wrath that sergeant cannot stifle,
He grabs a private's dirty rifle.
"The Colonel will see this," he raves.
But over it his wand Dan waves.

But now you're in for some good fun,
That rifle's now a water-gun.
The water shoots all o'er the place,
But most lands on the Colonel's face.

The Colonel doesn't stop to think—
He sends that lad straight off to clink.
The other soldiers ain't half happy
To get rid of that nasty chappie!

19

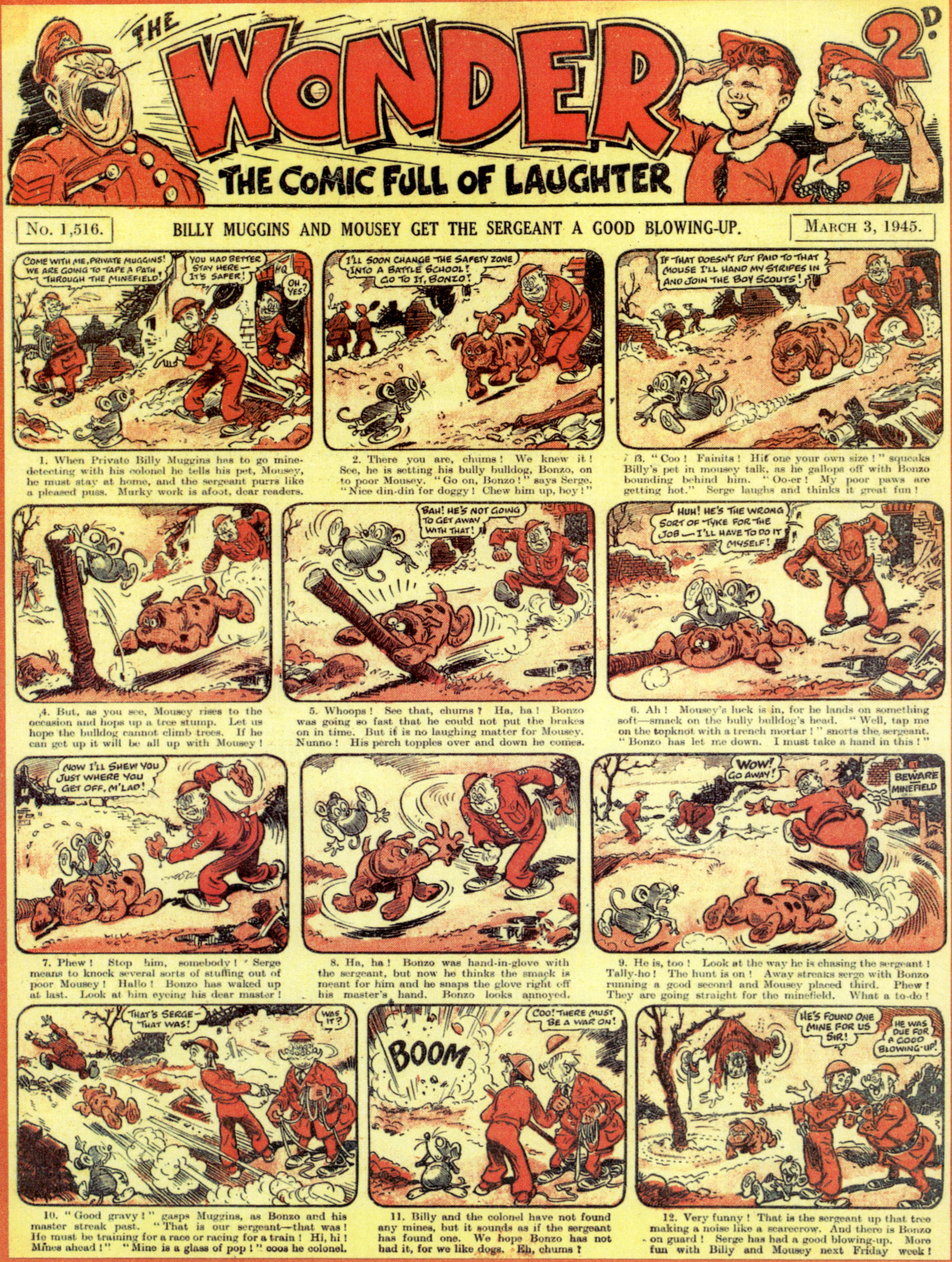

Bandy Legs; Magic; November 1940; (Roland Davies); © D.C. Thomson.

Koko the Pup; Magic; September 1940; (James Crichton); © D.C. Thomson.

 # CINDERELLA and Her ARTFUL SISTERS

Cinderella; Jester; November 1939; (Reg Parlett); © Amalgamated Press.

Homeless Hector, the Tail of a Lost Dog

1. Hector was made military mascot and looked a bit of all right, too. But Sergeant Slingem gave three jeers for the new recruit. "What a sight!" he cackled.

2. "Grr! Laugh at someone your own size!" barked our bow-wow, and he made a charge, catching the sniggering sergy in the waistcoat, pushing him back.

3. Sergy Slingem made a counter attack and grabbed at Hecky, thus flicking off the window-sill of the cookhouse a large and tasty-looking army pie. Fact!

4. So a bit of something good came Hector's way after all, and Sergy Slingem collected a rousing wallop from the cook's rolling-pin. Tuck in Hecky! 18-5-40

Homeless Hector; Chips; May 1940; (Arthur Martin); © Amalgamated Press.

Casey Court; Chips; November 1940; (Albert Pease); © Amalgamated Press.

This week, with the kind assistance of our tame artist, we give you a widespread eyeful of the Casey Court Soldiers' Club, which you will agree is just the stuff to give the troops. Here the gallant lads can get cared for more than they jolly well care for. All kinds of fun and games are provided, together with discomforts of every kind. Buttons and boots can be polished up, and grub can be polished off. There's an entertainment department and a bedtime-story bureau where tired warriors can be soothed off to slumber. Rifles are cleaned and completely ruined free of all charge, and there's a special device for helping soldiers to raise their battle bowlers. Mr. William Baggs, the manager and secretary, offers a hearty welcome to all units in tunics.

TANKS A MILLION!

What would the Army have done without the Tank Corps? We may never know. But what comics would have done without tanks is obvious: they wouldn't have been half so comical, as can be clearly seen from this parade of pictorial percussion. And if there had not been real tanks for the likes of Our Ernie ('Mrs Entwhistle's Little Lad') and Handy Andy the Odd-Job Man to cock-up in **Knockout,** then they would have to have invented them. Which is roughly what Our Gang did in D. Watkins' version of the Hal Roach films as depicted in the **Dandy.** Tiger Tim and the Bruin Boys, famous front page animals since **Rainbow** began in 1914, also built their own tank in one of these nursery heroes' rare brushes with wartime reality.

Tiger Tim; Tiger Tim's Weekly; April 1940; (Artist Unknown); © Amalgamated Press.

> "GOODNESS. THERE WILL BE A SPLASH IN A MINUTE!"
>
> "HI! THIS IS NOT A WATER TANK!"
>
> TIGER TIM'S TANK

Rumble! Rumble! Goodness, look! Tim has made a "tank" with the garden rollers and the boys are going for a trip. But, oh dear! The duck pond is in the way, and it seems they will all soon be going for a dip, too! Oo-ops! SPLASH!

Hairy Dan; Beano; January 1944; (Basil Blackaller); © D.C. Thomson.

HAIRY DAN— Brains our Hairy doesn't lack—See him mend that broken track!

Stymie and his Magic Wishbone; Radio Fun; November 1941; (Roy Wilson); © Amalgamated Press.

1. Our little coal-coloured comic was feeling tired in the tootsies, and thinking he would like a ride he wished for something on wheels. Promptly his magic Wishbone did its stuff and Stymie found himself dressed up as a nursemaid pushing a pramful of little Soccer students—otherwise two infants on the bawl. But he soon got rid of them and their noise, and then, seeing a poster about a tank demonstration, he wished another wish.

2. And in a brace of jiffies there he was packed in an old water tank that was parked on an old-iron man's barrow. "Hi, golly—you'se got me all wrong again, Wishbone," stuttered Stymie. "Dis ain't a Waltzing Matilda." However, he got a free ride to the common and there he saw a fine tank cavorting about. "Oho, so dis lubly tank captures batteries of guns, does it," mused Stymie. "Dat's fine! I wish we could see de batteries."

3. Oh dear, oh goodness gracious—Wishbone has done its stuff all wrong again. Everybody WAS surprised when they saw a flock of small dry batteries, and some wet ones as well, prancing about. "We're not afraid of any old tank," they crackled. Stymie hastily had them wafted away, and then the little lad wafted himself round to the camp, where he saw some soldiers having their afternoon nap after their knife-and-fork drill.

4. Well, as they wouldn't rise for their sergeant our Stymie treated himself to another wish and those soldiers rose all right then. Oh yes! And they were astonished when they found themselves floating about in the air on their beds. "Oh goody-goody," crowed the sergeant. "Got 'em up at last—and they can stay up while I take you to the canteen for a cup o' cocoa and a couple of cakes, Stymie." "T'ank you, sah," said Stymie.

Willie and Tim; Chips; May 1940; (Percy Cocking); © Amalgamated Press.

[No. 2,591.] **WEARY WILLIE AND TIRED TIM, THE WORLD-FAMOUS FUN STARS.** [May 4, 1940.]

1. Hallo, Chipites!—Here's your old pal, the Editor, telling you the latest episode in the history of Willie and Tim, the roaming rib-ticklers. Well, when they spotted a lorry loaded with tin tuck, Willie used his head and another lump of wood.

2. The result was that the lorry did a bump and out bounced a flock of canned comforts. "What-ho!" whooped Willie. "I like my grub wrapped up in tin overcoats!" "Too true!" tuffed Tim. "I can see where our next meal is coming from!"

3. Well, soon everything was set out for a set to. "With the aid of my penknife I will now open the tins and sharpen up my appetite!" tootled Tim. "Every tin is a round meal, except the sardine hangar, and that's a square 'un! Ha, ha!"

4. At this moment a bit of a surprise came to our playchums, and it came in the shape of a ten-ton tank, which was out on a bit of hedge-hopping practice. "Hey, here comes the iron terror!" woozed Willie. "Call up Dane, the Dog Detective!"

5. But the terror passed, and as it ambled peacefully on its way it left behind it the flattened-out remains of the tin tuck. "Well, soak me with soda!" gulped Tim. "Our iron rations have been ironed out, and that's flat, chum!"

6. And so with sorrow in their hearts and grubless 'neath their waistcoats, they set forth in the hope of getting something else to put on the menu. "There must be a camp near here!" puffed Willie. "We'll come to the cookhouse door!"

7. Everything turned out nice again, too, and they jolly soon kidnapped some more tinned tasties. But before they could quite get away they heard the sound of footmarks.

8. So, with great presence of mind-your-own-business, they bunged the grub into the barrel of a nought-point-nought howitzer. "I wonder howitzer going to work," sniffed Tim.

9. Then up came Gunner Gumboil, who was an expert gun-tester, having started his apprenticeship as a water-pistol squasher. "I'll give this gun the once-off!" said he to him.

10. So he went to the blunt end where the works are kept and pulled the gadget which caused a blank shell to make our pair wonder where their next meal was suddenly going to!

11. "Crumbs, our grub's gone off with a bang!" boodled Tim. "After it, Willie!" "You bet!" wheezed Willie. "This is a quickfire lunch, and I don't like to bolt my food, even if I have to bolt for it! Beat the barrage, matey!"

12. Well, the grub came to rest after a bit and it didn't seem much worse for the trip. "Cooluvalollipop!" panted Tim. "It's made a happy landing, and I bet it's nicely warmed up by now! I know our hopes would not be crushed, Willie!"

13. But the grub was, for at that jiff the tank did a come-back and another meal went flat. So our artful grub-grabbers swooned and they had to make do with a couple of mouthfuls of fresh air and a walk for dinner.—Thine, CORNY CHIPS.

Handy Andy; Knock-Out; September 1942; (A.J. Kelly); © Amalgamated Press.

HANDY ANDY - THE ODD JOB MAN

Casey Court; Chips; April 1940; (Albert Pease); © Amalgamated Press.

1. Kit and Kingy toddled out the other day to pick apple happily, but Whizzy was first!
2. There he was, scrumping in the royal applery, so Kingy set his Peck-at-Ease at him!
3. Whizzy felt pained in the pants, and limped home, vowing to get quits with our pals.

4. He made himself a Wall-busting Tank and started back for Kongo Kourt fruiteries.
5. He guessed Kit and Kingy would be watching the wall, but that wall wasn't there long.
6. Whizzy's tank bent it quite a bit, and then safe from the poodle, the Brit-bashers scrumped.

7. Oodles of apples and pints of pippins they piled in the tank, and rumbled back home.
8. But they'd seen plums in the royal orchard, too, and thought it 'ud be easy to pinch 'em.
9. But Kit guessed they'd come plumb after the plums and waited for them with a big stick.

10. How Whizzy laffed! He reckoned Kit's stick was no use against a tin-plated tank!
11. But Kit hooked up the royal manhole cover and made an opening for three bad lads!
12. Whizzy and his Brit-bashers went conk on the coke in the koal-hoal. Serve 'em right!

Stonehenge Kit; Knock-Out; July 1943; (A.J. Kelly); © Amalgamated Press.

The Gangsters Soon'll Have Wet Coats—When They Build a Tank That Floats!

OUR GANG

These boys and girls play in the famous Hal Roach Films of "Our Gang" and appear here by courtesy of M-G-M.

PETE THE PUP | ALFALFA SWITZER | SCOTTY BECKETT | DARLA HOOD | BILLY THOMAS | PATSY MAY | PORKY LEE | SPANKY McFARLAND | BUCKWHEAT THOMAS

1—After a week's hard saving Our Gang were able to afford to go to the pictures. There they saw a floating tank, and so they decided to build one.

2—So after the show was finished they started collecting material to make a tank. Porky Lee's contribution was one nail, one hammer, and a pot of glue!

3—They had their tank built in no time, then went away to feed their faces. The Kelly Gang were very jealous, and filled Our Gang's tank with stones.

4—After dinner Our Gang got into their tank and scudded downhill to the river to test their latest invention. The Kellyites watched all this gleefully.

5—Splash! Our Gang's tank hit the water. The Gangsters didn't have to wait long to know if it would sink or float. It sank like a stone.

6—It took Alfalfa some time to recover from the shock. Another of his ideas had failed. "Ha! Ha!" yelled the Kellyites, "we made your tank sink!"

7—After Our Gang had dried their clothes they salvaged their tank. Porky was determined to teach the Kellies a lesson, because his nail was all rusty.

8—An hour later the Kelly Gang came along and saw the tank lying in the middle of a meadow, so they climbed inside to have a look at it.

9—When they got inside they decided to have a nap. While Scotty screwed them in, Alfalfa and Porky got to work with a paint brush.

10—When the Kellyites woke up they saw a lot of ugly-looking fish. This was what the Gangsters had painted to bluff their rivals that they were below the sea.

11—The Kelly Gang were very scared, and started yelling for help. Little did they know that they were in the centre of the town and were the star attraction of Our Gang's Lifeboat Fund. Because of Our Gang's paint-brush tricks they weren't able to hold their heads up for weeks after.

Our Ernie; Knock-out; March 1940; (Hugh McNeill); © Amalgamated Press.

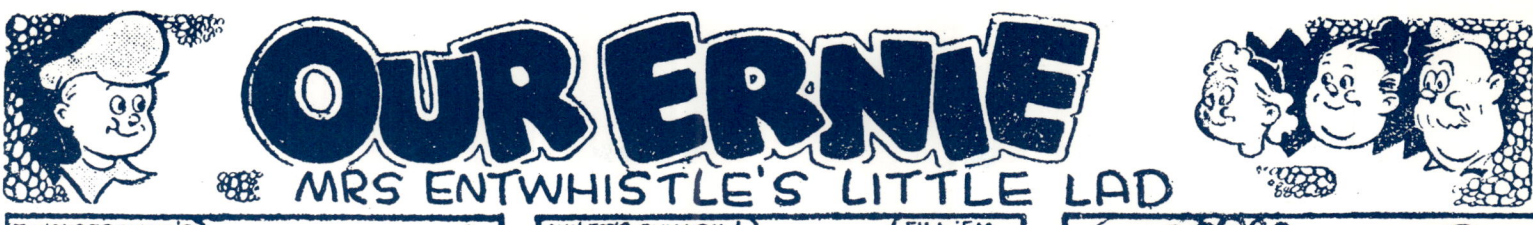

OUR ERNIE
MRS ENTWHISTLE'S LITTLE LAD

There's soljers down our Ernie's way,
And so our lad, the other day,
Said to himself, "Yon soldiers' camp
Should be good fun!" The little scamp!

"FOR TANKS" were painted on a drum,
And little Ernie thought "By gum—
I wonder what's for tanks in there,
It must be summat strange and rare."

Well, lad climbed right up to the top,
And at the top the lad did stop,
For after all his pain and toil,
All that were in the drum were oil.

Just then some soljers working there,
Grabbed hold of drum without a care,
They'd cum to take the thing away,
And Ernie fell in, sad to say.

Now oil were thick, and black, and gooey,
And Ernie got all Bug-a-booey,
So when into a tank they shot him,
The soljers ran, when they did spot him.

Well, after this, tank rolled away,
Thought lad: "I'm stuck here for the day,
My mother will be cross with me—
By gum—suppose I miss my tea!"

The tank pushed down a house or two
(There isn't much they won't go through),
Then to edge of cliff it rumbled,
And o'er the edge it swiftly tumbled.

Into the water tank did go
And squashed a U-boat there below,
Thought Ernie: "That's one up to me—
He won't sink no more Nootral ships—you see!"

Next lad ran into Oc-tow-puss,
And Oc-tow-puss did make a fuss,
He's got eight legs, and so you see,
Four times as many corns as me!

That Oc-tow-puss fair swelled with wrath,
And smacked the tank for all 'twas worth.
He kicked it with three legs together,
Three legs as tough as toughest leather.

The tank was smacked right out of water
And flew much further than it oughter.
It flew right over fields and houses,
And birds and cows and rats and mouses.

Near Ernie's house it hit the ground
And shook the land for miles around,
While voice from hole, as wee as wee,
Cried: "Wotcher, ma—throw down my tea."

AT SEA WITH THE NAVY!

It is natural that an island nation should crew its comics with merry mariners and saucy seadogs. Thus we have Jolly Jack Robinson duffing up the Japs and the Russkis in **Merry & Bright** back in 1904, the same year that Jack B. Yeats drew Sandab the Sailor in **Puck**. Pitch and Toss shipped aboard **Funny Wonder** in 1922, sailed over to the front page in 1932, and despite their merchant mariner status, did their fat and thin bits to blow the Bosche to the bloaters once the war came round. Their artist, the brilliant Roy Wilson, also drew the naval nonsenses of Lieutenant Daring and Jolly Roger, 'The Bold Sea Rovers' of **Golden**. Hairy Dan, 'Whose Whiskers Neat Reach to His Feet' in **Beano**, joined the Navy and served almost alongside Rip Van Wink, that comic's old codger who found life a bit baffling after his 700-year sleep.

Casey Court; Chips; December 1939; (Albert Pease); © Amalgamated Press.

Rip Van Wink; Beano; August 1942; (James Crichton); © D.C. Thomson.

1. Dear old Addy had cleverly fallen asleep without falling out of his hammock, and Roger was busy polishing the deck, when a visitor dropped in on them.

2. Yes, Goldens. A sly nasty spy came down from an aeroplane, making a noise like a fairy, and he calmly proceeded to borrow Addy's best secret plans.

3. "Help-pelp! Up the navy!" piped Roger. "What's wrong?" cried the lieutenant. "Look!" sang Roger. "That man is giving Addy a nasty turn!"

 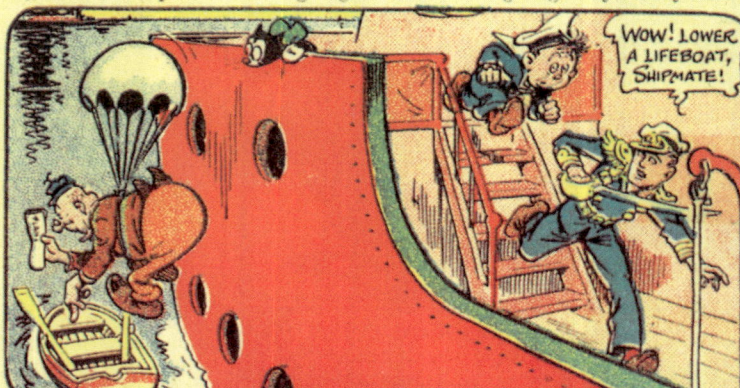

4. True enough, the spy gave Addy such a bad "turn" that he left him feeling quite tied up. Then, leaping over Roger, the visitor took his leave. But Daring meant to stop him taking those plans. "Ooh! He's got me down!" cried Roger.

5. "Ho, ho, ho! I haff der plans and avay I go!" sang Hans Hoff, the nasty spy, as he did a fairy-like flip down to his waiting boat. "What's to do, sir!" cried Roger "Lower a lifeboat, quick!" replied the lively lieutenant.

6. So the wee sailor-lad leaped overboard, and as Daring followed him over the side he neatly cut the ropes. "A short 'cut' for us, boy!" he cried.

7. But you should always look before you leap, our heroes learned too late. For it wasn't a lifeboat at all. It was just a workman's cradle. See?

8. "Shiver my main-braces!" gasped Roger in dismay. "We have let ourselves in for something, sir!" Luckily they landed on a giant bloater, below.

9. "Hurrah! It is taking us for a ride, sir!" cried Roger as the big fish set off after Hans Hoff. "Ach! Der British Navy iss everywhere!" said that scared spy. Then the big fish gave a friendly flip with his tail and sent our bold sea rovers sailing into the spy's boat. "Got you!" cried Daring.

10. "Hip-pip-pooray!" cheered Roger. "We take the plans and upset his plans, sir! Nice work!" "Bah!" hooted Hans. "You iss der pain in der neck to me!" "Sorry if I'm putting a crease in your collar-stud!" chuckled Roger. "But duty is duty!" And wasn't Addy pleased to see his plans back!

Lt. Daring and Jolly Roger; Golden; February 1940; (Roy Wilson); © Amalgamated Press.

"KNOCK-OUT" COMIC
BILLY BUNTER
THE FATTEST SCHOOLBOY ON EARTH!

Billy Bunter; Knock-Out; July 1942; (Frank Minnitt); © Amalgamated Press.

Our Ernie; Knock-Out; September 1942; (Fred Robinson); © Amalgamated Press.

Rowing out on foam one day,
What should lad spot in Wigan Bay,
But man-o'-war, so trim and neat—
A solid lump of British Fleet.

"By gum!" cried lad, "I'll row alongside
'Cos British Fleet is Wigan's pride,
And if Admiral is local lad,
I'll give him love from ma and dad!"

But before lad could ask for skipper's name,
Out from the side of ship there came
A spout of water, cold and dank,
And into the waves poor Ernie sank.

But Admiral, a decent sort,
Crossing from starboard side to port,
Saw Ernie struggling in the gravy,
And cried, "O.K., lad. We can save 'ee!"

So lad were hoisted up on high,
Where sailor boys soon rubbed him dry,
And Admiral said he would be glad,
To lend spare suit to little lad.

"By gum!" cried lad. "I'm lucky. Eeh!
Now I'm an Admiral in King's Navee!
I think I'll take a stroll about
Finding gadgets and trying 'em out!"

So pressing this and pulling that,
(Including tail of skipper's cat),
Lad danced the ship around so quick,
The crew complained they felt sea-sick.

When lad left ship he didn't know,
Quite what it were that made him go,
He pressed a button and took a chance,
And sea-plane hit him in the pants!

And so he sailed through sky of blue,
And looking down to get the view,
What should he spot but E-boat crew,
Using our sea to sail in, too!

"Of all the cheek!" cried lad. "Here goes!
I'll pull that Nasti skipper's nose!
I'll make him dance, and hop and skip!
By gum! I think I'll pinch his ship!"

So that's how Ernie got to be,
Admiral of his own Navee,
While poor old Charlie had to do
Work of officers and crew.

And Admiral signalled as lad sped by,
"Where are you off to, son, and why?"
Back came the signal from brave Ernie,
"What d'you think, pal? Home for tea!"

Hairy Dan; Beano; June 1943; (Basil Blackaller); © D.C. Thomson.

Hairy Dan; Beano; July 1943; (Basil Blackaller); © D.C. Thomson.

Pitch and Toss; Funny Wonder; May 1941; (Roy Wilson); © Amalgamated Press.

SINKING THE SUBS!

U-boats, those undersea sardine-tins from World War One, surfaced again in World War Two, packed to the portholes with nasty Nazis only too eager to toss off a torpedo or ten at Our Brave Lads. Tables, and torpedoes, were swiftly turned by the likes of Alfie the Air Tramp and his Spare Part, Wagger the Skye-Terrier and, oddly, Pansy Potter. **The Beano's** famous Strong Man's Daughter seemed to make U-boat sinking her speciality, as shall be shown when we arrive in due course at our special section devoted to the distaff department. Meanwhile, over in **The Dandy**, Desperate Dan joined the Navy – whether the British, the Canadian, the American or the Cactusville is unclear – and made a characteristic start on the subs. Our Ernie of the **Knockout,** came off best, however, as accompanied by the ever-present Charlie the Caterpillar he encountered not just U-boats but V-boats as well!

Our Ernie; Knock-Out; September 1941; (Frank Lazenby); © Amalgamated Press.

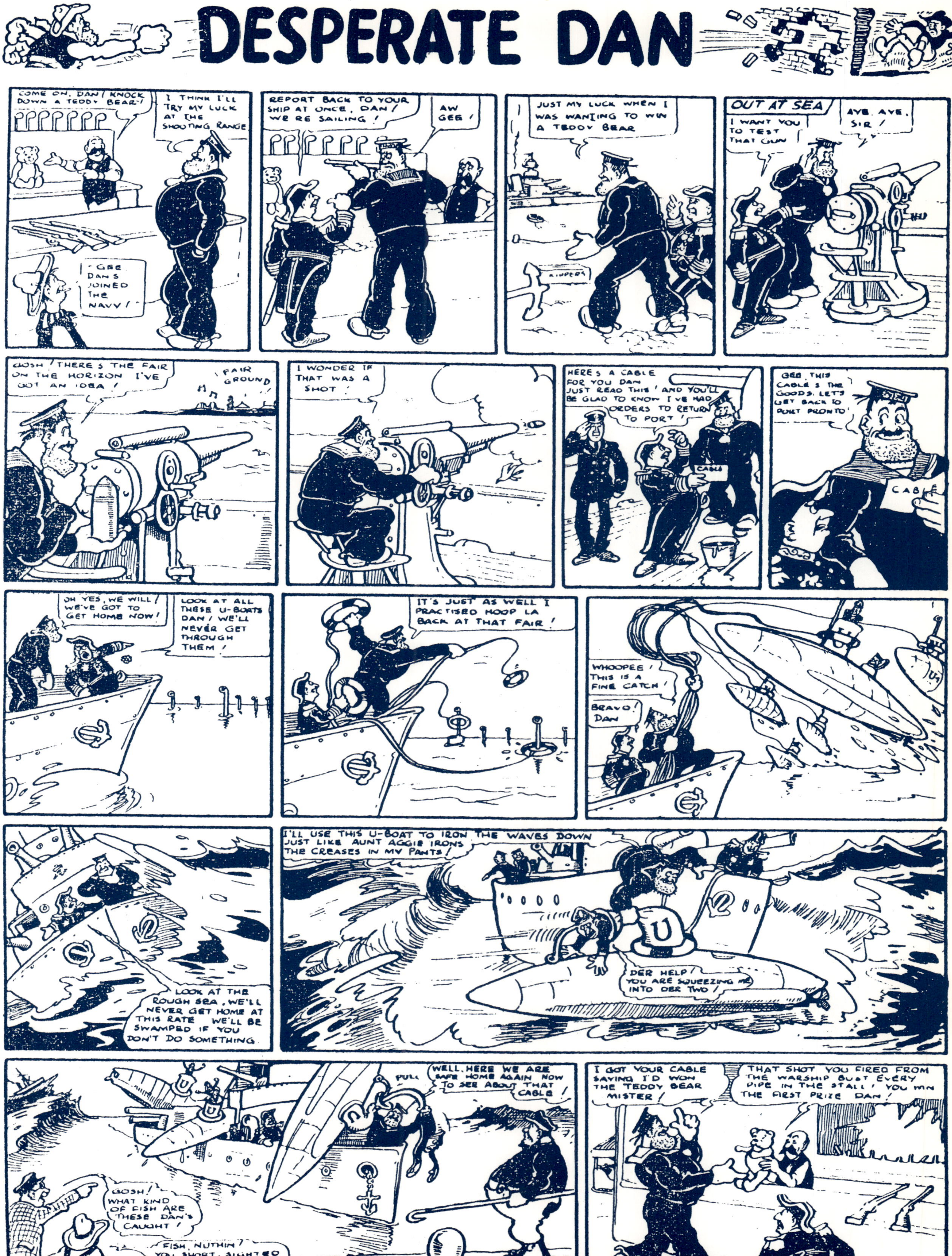

Desperate Dan; Dandy; June 1941; (Dudley Watkins); © D.C. Thomson.

Koko the Pup; Magic; November 1940; (Jack Crichton); © D.C. Thomson.

Alfie the Air Tramp; Chips; August 1941; (John Jukes); © Amalgamated Press.

Pansy Potter; Beano; September 1943; (Basil Blackaller); © D.C. Thomson.

1. The rations at Greyfriars were wearing a bit thin and getting frayed at the edges, chums, so Quelchy took the lads fishing, hoping to get a couple of cod, several salmon, and half as many haddocks. 'Twas better than sums, chums !

2. The lads properly enjoyed themselves—all except Billy Bunter. Even drowning a worm on the end of a line seemed like work, to him. His arms ached something awful, holding the rod. He reckoned the fish ought to have surrendered.

3. He was fed up with the whole business, and he hated it worse when Bob Cherry slapped him on the nose with a smelly smelt. Flap, it went, and Billy got annoyed. "I just won't fish, now," he barked, and sought a way of escape.

4. He found it ! The mighty Bunter brain sizzled once more. "I know ! " he grinned to himself. "I'll kip, and the other rotters can do the kippering." So he made himself comfy.

5. No one bothered about him and he bothered about no one, like the rotten old miller of rotten Dee you've read about. But even a kip, like a kipper, has an end. Our fat lad woke up !

6. And there he was—gone to sea ! All, all alone, he was, on the rotten old heaving ocean, like a rotten old castaway. At least, he thought he was alone until the convoy butted in !

7. Before Billy knew what was which, there were wallops of bangs and shells flying all round him. His punt stopped a fourpenny one somewhere abaft the beam behind the binnacle beside the bilge. And things came unstuck.

8. Billy wanted to get out of the punt, but he didn't have to worry. Another iron ration simply blew him into the drink—and it wasn't grapefruit either ! Bang, whistle, whee-ee, went the shells. And splosh went Billy Bunter.

9. The sad sea waves swallowed him up, but they didn't like him much, for they tossed him up again—pants first ! A. P. Tuffensalt reported a floating mine off the offing, bu tthe escort ships were too busy to bother about it just then.

10. And Billy swum and swam and swum and swam till his senses were swimming. And just when he thought he was water-lgoged he spotted a stick sticking up in the water. Never before in his fat life had he wanted the stick !

11. Swimming, swumming, and swamming, he reached the stick and climbed up it out of the damp wetness. And things began to happen. The higher he climbed the higher went the stick. Up and up went Billy, and up went the stick.

12. And then, Billy cast a terrified gaze down beneath him. It fell flop on the deck of a Nasti U-boat, which took him so by surprise that he slid down the stick to the slippery ship. And Kapitan Karl Hottenadogger didn't like it.

13. He thought our fat lad was a spy. "Take-heem below, wasn't it!" he growled. And the Nasti seamen tried hard to obey, but it was no go, at all. Square pegs won't fit in round holes, as they knew—but this was different!

14. This was a round chappy who wouldn't go in a round hole. Our Billy stuck tight in the hatch and wouldn't go to or come from. They tried pushing in and pulling out. They tried with a shoe-horn and a hammer. Nothing doing.

15. There was Billy, and that was that! And just then, a British sub-smasher steamed in sight. Kapitan Karl got the jitters and ordered a crash dive. "Those on deck must schwim, shouldn't it?" he yelled. Going down?

16. The U-boat went down, and what the Nasti sailors couldn't do the rush of wet sea-water did, easily. Billy shrunk in the wash and popped out of that hatch like a cork out of a bottle.

17. Coo, he was put out! Up he popped to the surface, his face washed by gallons of Channel. And just then the British boat dropped a depth charge. Billy looked just like a flying-fish!

18. Only he was plumper, perhaps. He came down plump on a swimming Nasti. What might have happened after that there is no telling. But luckily, the U-boat turned up.

19. Maybe Kapitan Karl wanted to know who was knocking. The Nasti U-boat crew swarmed out to man the guns, and Billy saw his chance. He was in that hatch again before anybody could say, "Heil, Bunter." And there he stuck!

20. Those Nasti sub-men didn't like it a little bit. They couldn't dodge inside their tin-boat again. Billy had them properly and barked orders. He made them scrub the decks and make things all ship-shape for the admiral.

21. The British sub-smasher came alongside and captured the U-boat. They towed it to jolly old England, but they had to get Billy out of the hatch, somehow, because the admiral wanted to see what was inside the U-boat.

22. So they rigged up a crane on the quay, and half the King's Navy did a heave-o, ah-hup, and blow, me bully boys, blow Billy out! Billy breathed out to make his waist waste, and out he came as slick as you like. Nice work!

23. And the admiral was pleased! "The Home Guard and the Sea Scouts are proud of you, my boy!" he said. "Not to mention the Navy." He wanted to know if there was anything he could do to make Billy comfortable.

24. Billy had had much pressure outside his waistline. He needed some pressure inside, now. So the Navy cooks got busy in the galley and came aft with the afters, popped up with the pop, and piped the grub aboard. Bully for Billy!

IN THE AIR WITH THE R.A.F.

One of the major mysteries of World War Two is why that well-known peacetime pilot, Alfie the Air Tramp, failed to enlist in the R.A.F. He was probably too fat to pass his medical – couldn't squeeze through the M.O.'s door! It was via the R.A.F. that war touched one of the nursery comics, as those papers published for the little Brits were labelled. Tiny and Tot, stars of **Tiny Tots**, were brought lit-tle un-i-forms by their Nur-sie, and had some hy-phen-a-ted ca-pers with their toy aer-o-planes. There was a lot more fun for the ten-year-olds when Fred Robinson began depicting those elfs of the airways, the Gremlins, in **Knockout**. Beginning as a strip, this series developed into the sort of big-picture prank that had been Casey Court's province for forty years.

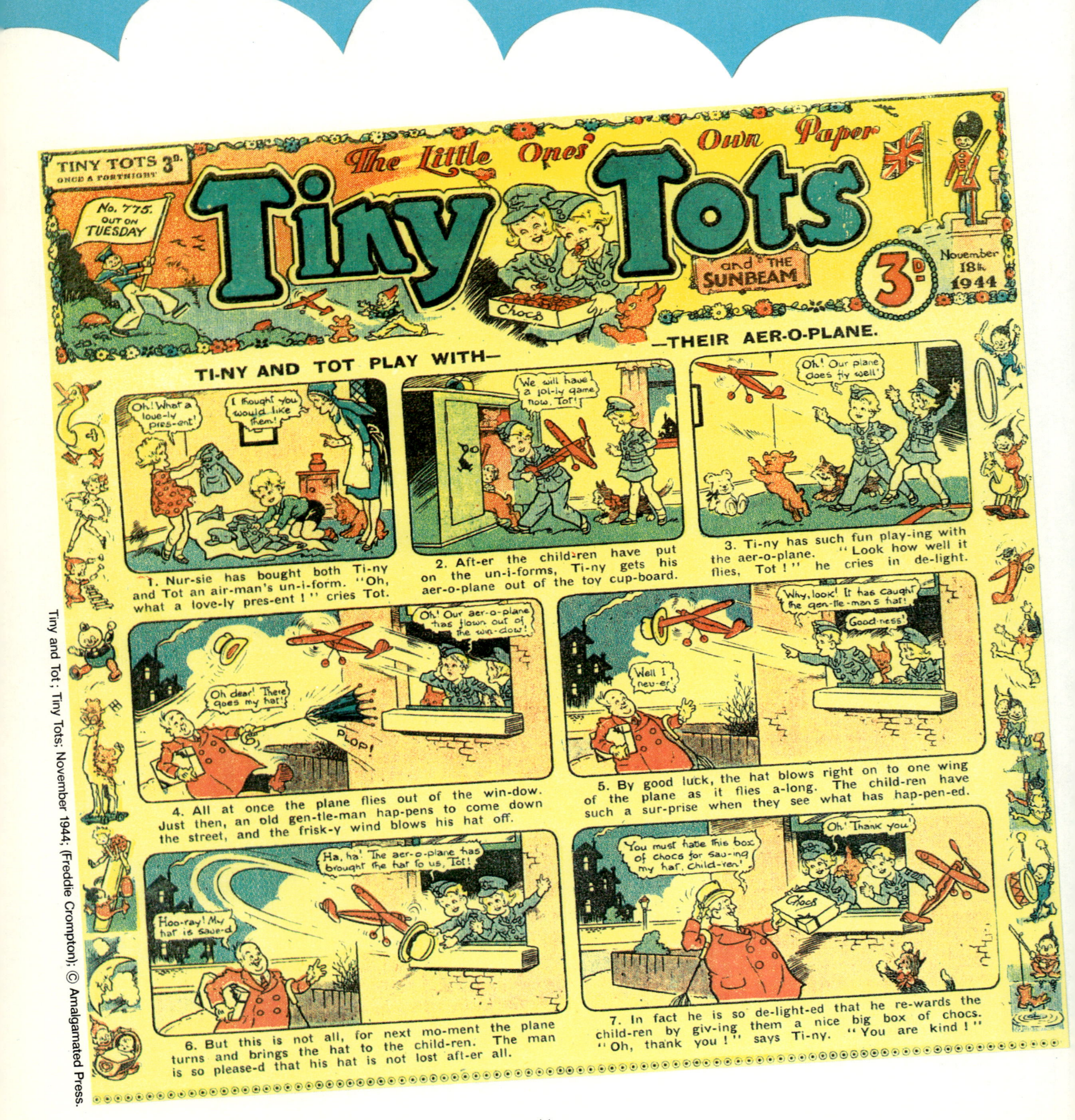

Tiny and Tot; Tiny Tots; November 1944; (Freddie Crompton); © Amalgamated Press.

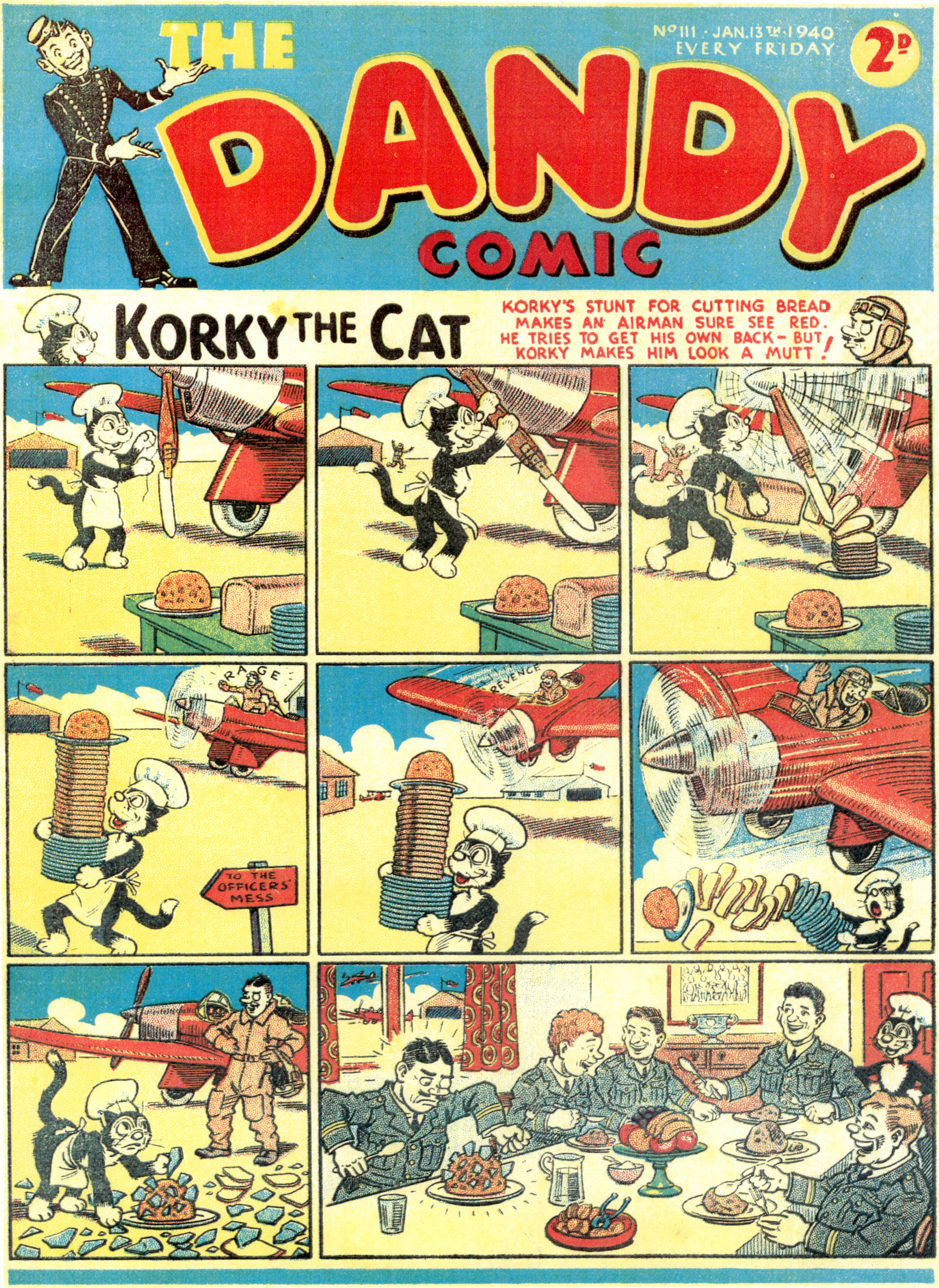

Korky the Cat: Dandy, January 1940; (James Crichton): © D.C. Thomson.

Gremlins; Knock-Out; January 1943; (Fred Robinson); © Amalgamated Press.

IT'S THE GREMLINS!

THE GREMLINS ARE THE ELFS OF THE AIR BUT PILOT OFFICER PLONK DIDN'T BELIEVE IN THEM. ONE DAY WHEN GURCH, THE GREMLIN WAS OUT FOR A WALK —

"WE'RE GLAD TO HAVE YOU WITH US PLONK, BUT I OUGHT TO WARN YOU THAT WE'RE PESTERED HERE BY THE GREMLINS."

"OH, I DON'T BELIEVE IN THAT BUNKUM SIR!"

"WELL, OF ALL THE NERVE!"

GREMLIN GRANGE

"LISTEN BOYS! THERE'S A NEW PILOT OFFICER JUST ABOUT TO TAKE OFF AND HE DOESN'T BELIEVE IN US!"

"WHAT SAUCE! LET'S GIVE HIM THE WORKS!"

"YOU HAVE YOUR INSTRUCTIONS, PLONK. NOW MIND THOSE GREMLINS!"

"TRUST ME SIR! BUT FORGET THE GREMLINS, THAT'S ALL HOOEY!"

1. Pilot-Officer Plonk wasn't at all a bad chap, but he thought an awful lot of himself. He reckoned he was a wow! He could fly anything, at any time and anyhow. So when he was posted to a new aerodrome and the squadron leader said they were pestered with Gremlins, he just gave a big laugh. "I don't believe in that bunkum, sir," he said. Unluckily for him, Gurch the Gremlin was standing behind a tuft of grass, listening.

"GREMLINS! — NEVER HEARD OF SUCH ROT!"

"YOU SOON WILL, YOU TWIRP!"

"WHAT'S THE MATTER WITH THIS CRATE?"

"COSH! I'VE GOT GREMLINS ON THE BRAIN! I'D BETTER GO DOWN!"

"HOW DO FELLAH?"
"YOO-HOO!"
"NICE WEATHER WE'RE HAVING!"
"NO COUPONS EITHER!"
"HOOEY AND BUNKUM, EH?"

2. "Of all the nerve!" he exclaimed angrily. And went dashing back home to Gremlin Grange. All his pals, his brothers, cousins and second-cousins were there. "Listen, boys!" he cried, leaping up on the table. "There's a new pilot officer here who doesn't believe in us!" Of course, that made the Gremlins sit up. They thought that everybody in the R.A.F. knew about them. They were always up to their pranks, night or day.

"I MUST BE GOING CRAZY! I DON'T BELIEVE THEY'RE REAL, I DON'T — I DON'T!"

"CLING TO HER NOSE BOYS! — HE'S TRYING TO LAND!"

"OW! I'M GOING TO CRASH! — I CAN'T PULL HER OUT OF THE DIVE!"

"TOO TRUE, YOU CAN'T BROTHER!"

3. Like Plonk, himself, they weren't such bad sorts, but they did like their little jokes. And for anybody to say they didn't even exist—well, it got their dander up. "We'll teach him a thing or two!" they chortled, looking forward to the fun. So they followed Gurch out on to the aerodrome, and there was Plonk climbing into his plane. "Gremlins!" he was muttering. "I never heard of such rot!" How the Gremlins chuckled!

"THAT'S TORN IT! NOW I'M FOR IT! AND IT WAS ALL THE FAULT OF THOSE GREMLINS."

"HEE HEE HEE! THAT WAS GOOD! WE'LL PLAY ANOTHER TRICK ON THAT TWIRP TOMORROW. — YOU SEE!"

"IT WASN'T MY FAULT SIR! THOSE GREMLINS GOT ME!"

"NONSENSE! YOU WERE FLYING LIKE A CLOWN! BESIDES YOU DON'T BELIEVE IN 'EM, — YOU SAID SO!"

4. They perched on his port wing, and tilted the machine. Plonk struggled vainly with the controls. Then he saw Gurch and his pals grinning at him. "I don't believe it!" he cried. He put his machine's nose down. Gurch and his pals rushed to the nose and Plonk was helpless. He crashed! And the Gremlins fled. Poor old Plonk. The squadron leader made it hot for him. And the Gremlins will teach him some more, next week.

46

Gremlins; Knock-Out; February 1943; (Fred Robinson); © Amalgamated Press.

IT'S THE GREMLINS!

1. Pilot-Officer Plonk had refused to believe there were such things as Gremlins until they had started playing their tricks on him. They gave him quite a headache, but there was no ill-feeling with Plonk. In fact, he had actually saved Gurch, the Gremlin, from a nasty bump when a Jerry bullet punctured his wings. After that, the Gremlins were pally with Plonk. The Adjutant, on the other hand, knew the Gremlins and hated them.

2. Of course, you cannot always see the Gremlins. If they don't want to be seen they can be pretty quick getting out of sight. But Gurch wasn't worrying about anything. He was sitting on a post sunning himself when the Adjutant handed him a fourpenny one, for nothing at all. The Adjutant was ordering his plane to be made ready for a flight. A nasty bit of work, he was, and Gurch liked nothing better than handling that sort.

3. So, after the mechanics had put the plane in order, Gurch called up his Gremlins and got busy on the Adjutant's crate. They knew all about planes and what shouldn't be done to them. They put water in the petrol tank. They cut chunks out of the wings and drew rude pictures on the fuselage. They tied the tail plane to the water stand-pipe. Everything was all ready for the Adjutant!

4. The Adjutant took off all right. Then the plane took off—in several pieces. The stand-pipe was busted. The engine came apart and the plane crashed right in front of the Squadron-Leader. Of course, the Adjutant blamed the Gremlins, but that excuse didn't get him anywhere. He saw what he thought was Gurch and heaved a brick at him, smashing Squaddy's window. So the Gremlins won! Don't miss their pranks, next week.

THE MAGIC COMIC

N° 33 · 2ⁿᵈ MAR · 1940
EVERY THURSDAY

KOKO the PUP

BY PARACHUTE, POOR KOKO'S DROPPED.
IN SPLOSHY-SPLASHY MUD HE'S FLOPPED.
THE AIRMEN LAUGH, BUT HE LAUGHS LAST—
TO SEE THEIR PANTS FLY ON THE MAST.

AWFUL ADOLF AND HIS NASTY NAZIS!

'Know Your Enemy' was the kind of Ministry of Information motto that nobody needed, certainly not the comic-reading crowd. The boys and girls of Britain were well prepared, thanks to Basil and Bert of **The Jester,** and once war had been well and truly declared, the Nasty Nazis were fair game for fun. Whether he was called Awful Adolf, Old 'Itler, Tickler, Old Man Schickelgrubb (in the comedy song by Leslie Sarony), Old Nasti, Der Foorer, he was just plain Hitler to Lord Snooty and his Pals who survived a memorable encounter with him and were rewarded by a cheer from Churchill! **The Dandy** actually starred the Reischschancellor himself and his right-hand man, Field Marshal Goering, as a double-act called Addie and Hermy the Nasty Nazis!

Once again Lord Snooty and his Pals were well to the fore in their classic encounter with Benito Mussolini: they quickly put the ill into il Duce! But it would be **The Beano** this time that turned the facist dictator into a comic strip star, giving him the well-remembered title of 'Musso the Wop – He's a Big-a-da Flop'!

'Slap the Japs' was an All-American edict that found echoes in the pages of British comics. Big Eggo **The Beano's** big bird, was no racist: he dealt with Japs as cheerfully as he did Jerries and Eye-ties!

Addy and Hermy; Dandy; January 1940; (Sam Fair); © D.C. Thomson.

Our Ernie; Knock-Out; June 1940; (Hugh McNeill); © Amalgamated Press.

OUR ERNIE
MRS. ENTWHISTLE'S LITTLE LAD.

Like other kids, Our Ernie eats
A shocking awful lot of sweets,
So he was cross, was our young pup,
When war put price of lollies up.

"It's Tickler's fault!" the kids all cried,
Which made Our Ernie then decide,
To go and punch old Tickler's conk,
He meant to give it such a clonk.

With Charlie Caterpillar in his pocket
Lad did himself up in a packet,
And having posted him to France,
Our Lad began his big advance.

Two sojers then the boy unwropped,
And gasped two gasps when out he popped,
It really gave them quite a shock,
To see Our Ernie's smiling clock.

Well, off strode Ernie right away,
To punch old Tick without delay,
He thought it would be luvly fun,
To cop his conk a fourpenny wun.

Through No-Man's-Land Our Ernie stalked,
While Charlie just behind him walked,
With little gas mask in its box,
And all his feets in pale green sox.

Well, after walking miles and miles,
Our Ernie's face broke into smiles,
For he'd seen passage in the ground,
Through which old Tickler could be found.

At other end, lad had to larf,
He found old Tickler in his barf,
He looked a daffy sort of chap,
Wiv flag tied on his barf-room tap!

Our Ernie through the trap-door rose,
And clonked old Nasty on the nose,
Which made him say some naughty things,
Like "Spifflicate my thiggummy-jings!"

Then, just to show what he had done,
Young Ernie thought it would be fun,
To tug old Tickler's tash right out,
Then nobody his tale would doubt.

Disguised as Tickler with that Tash,
Through Germany lad made a dash,
And just caught troopship at the coast,
With room for wun more lad, at most.

And so back home Our Ernie came
Although he didn't look the same,
He cried: "Just give my tea to me—
I'M GOING TO INVADE IT—SEE?"

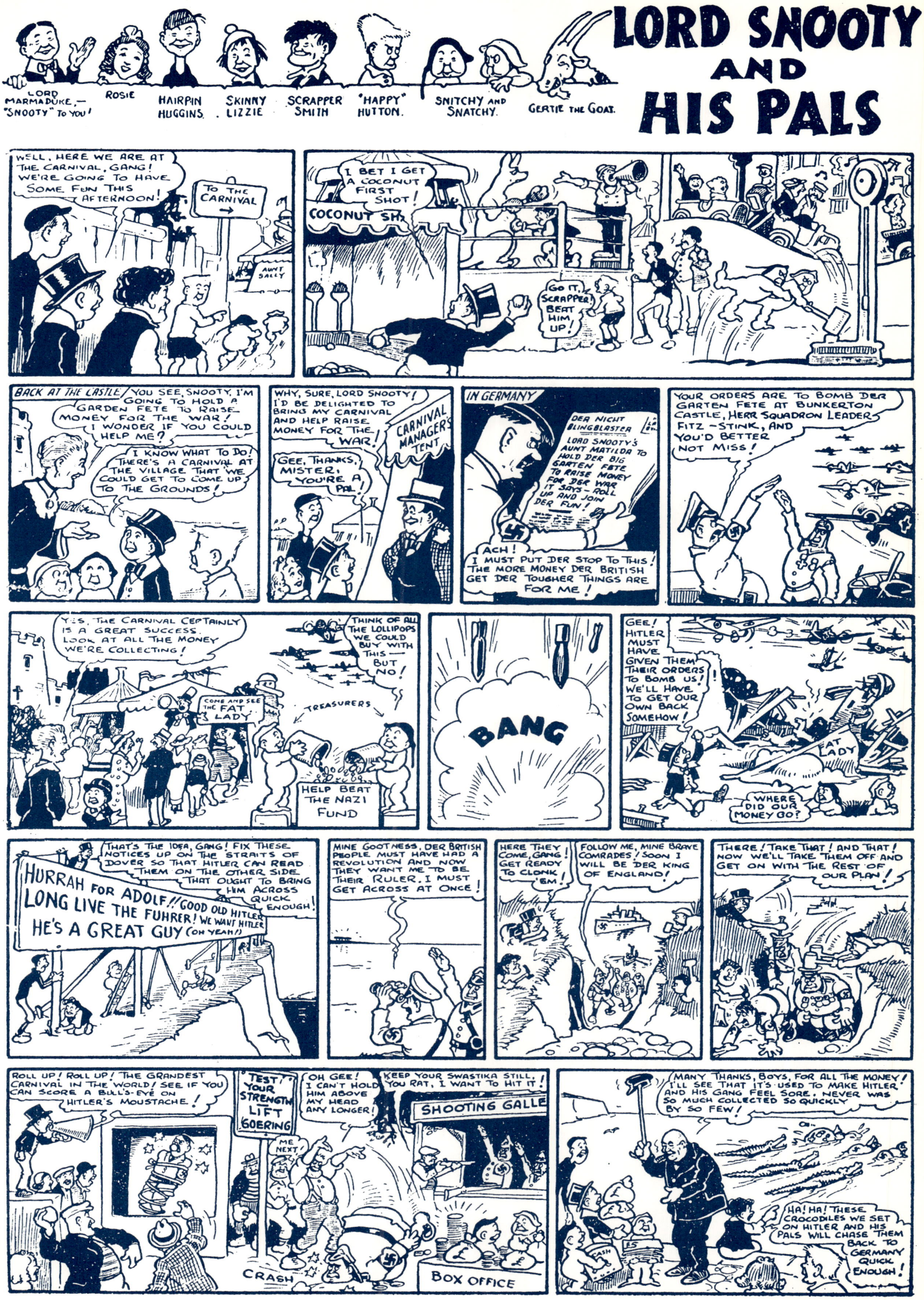

Lord Snooty; Beano; August 1942; (Dudley Watkins); © D.C. Thomson.

Pitch and Toss; Wonder; April 1943; (Roy Wilson); © Amalgamated Press.

Big Eggo; Beano; July 1940; (Reg Carter); © D.C. Thomson.

ADDIE AND HERMY THE NASTY NAZIS

Addy and Hermy; Dandy; December 1940; (Sam Fair); © D.C. Thomson.

Plum and Duff; Comic Cuts; April 1941; (Albert Pease); © Amalgamated Press.

PLUM and DUFF — THE BOYS OF THE BOLD BRIGADE

1. "That's torn it!" snorted Suet, as the Wop did a whiz off with his shaving brush and soap-pot. "I shan't be able to give my chin a once over now!"

2. "Cheer up, Sergy!" tooted Plum. "Perhaps summat will turn up!" But what did turn up was old Musso. What's more, he took a kick at the flag-pole and smashed it. "That's torn it!" snorted Plum.

3. But Musso hadn't finished yet. "I jumpa on da Union Jack!" he yapped. Duff was moving it slightly.

4. Yes, he pulled the flag along until it rested across the top of the well. Then the outsize macaroni muncher took a hop, skip, and a jump, fully intending to come down on the flag.

5. But he did nothing of the suchwhich. No, Duff deftly tugged it away smartly, and Musso saw the well for the first time. Also he flopped into it, fairly and squarely, and got firmly wedged. Wow!

6. He lost his ta-ta, too. So Plum picked it up and he snipped off the fancy trimming.

7. "Here you are, Sergy!" tooted the boys. "A nice smart shaving outfit for you!" So Suet thanked them and got on with the job of scraping his chin. Then up boodled Musso, looking very fierce.

8. He'd brought the well-top with him, and a pop-gun too. While he was holding up Sergy, Duff got busy with some paint and made a nobby dartboard.

9. And when the local nuts started playing, they soon saw old Musso off, to the delight of our heroes!

Our Ernie; Knock-Out; September 1942; (A.J. Kelly); © Amalgamated Press.

OUR ERNIE
MRS. ENTWHISTLE'S LITTLE LAD.

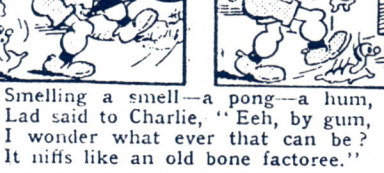

Smelling a smell—a pong—a hum,
Lad said to Charlie, "Eeh, by gum,
I wonder what ever that can be?
It niffs like an old bone factoree."

But 'twere an Army Cooking School,
Where they have queerest sort of rule,
That Concrete Mixers teach at courses
In cooking pudding for the Forces.

But when our young lad came in view,
They were cook short, so said "Hi! You!
For regiment you must make a pudden,
And mind! It's got to be a good 'un!"

Now being at school when ma was baking,
Our lad knew nowt of pudding making,
But did his best with stuff he could find,
And turned out pud. of quite new kind.

This pud. did everything but talk,
And when they prodded it with fork
It proved it were Commando pud.—
Tough and hard as lump of wood!

It bent the fork, and crumpled shell,
It smashed up hefty tank as well,
That pud. could take real punishment
And come out neither cracked nor bent.

Well, Army soon gave pudding best,
And sent attacking troops for rest,
When bomber pilot passing pud.
Cried, "Eeh, I'd like that there, I would!"

"It's just the thing, sir, as you'll see,
For us to take to Shermanee,
We'll carry it to old Berlin,
Where Tickler's due to make a din."

Cried Ernie, peering through the air,
"Eeh, there's old Nuisance standing there,
Get ready to let go the pud. !
It ought to do a bit of good!"

So down went pud. with rush and roar,
And nowt like it were seen before,
And folk with front seats at the show
Cried "Eeh, perhaps we'd better go!"

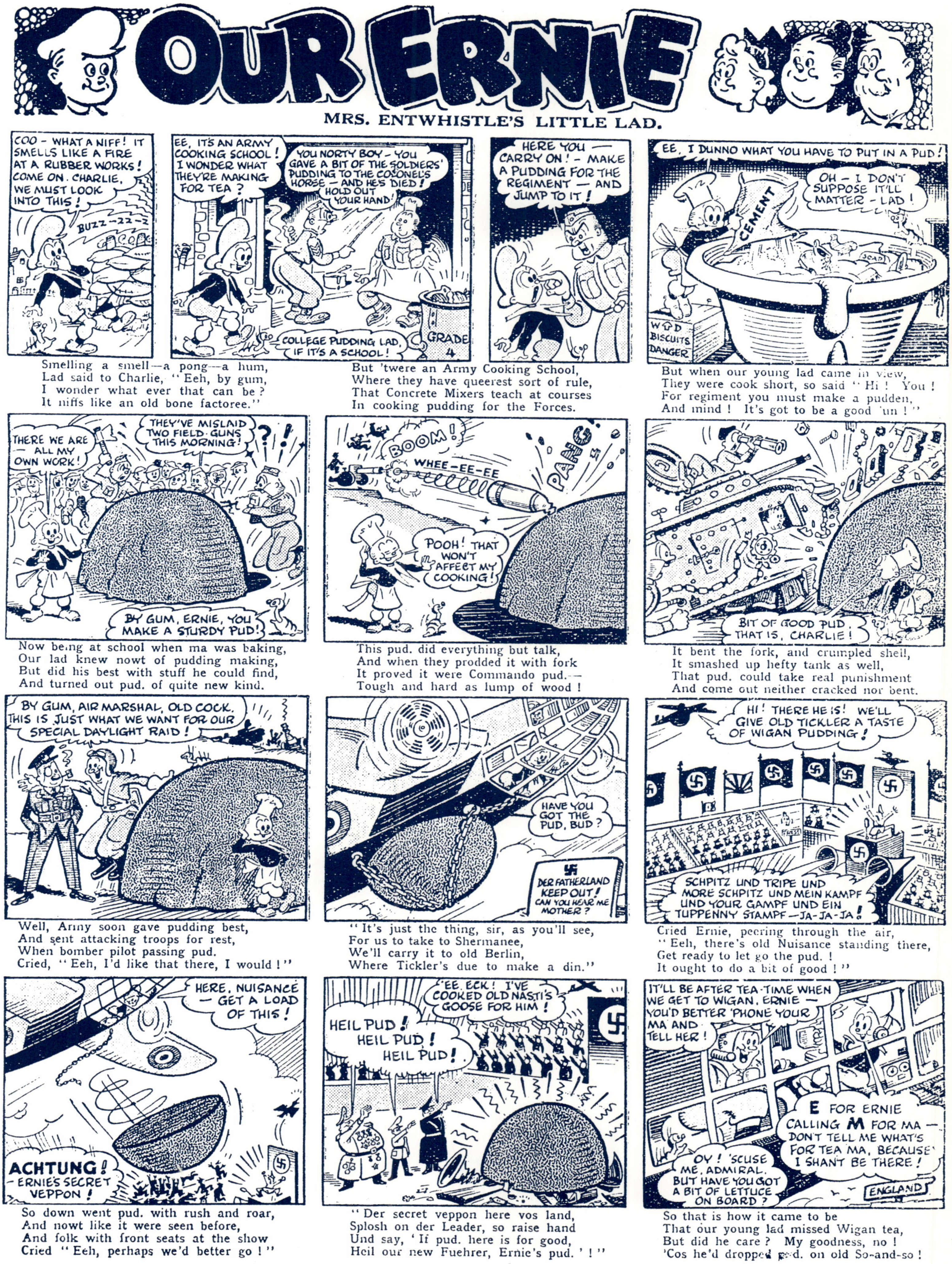

"Der secret veppon here vos land,
Splosh on der Leader, so raise hand
Und say, 'If pud. here is for good,
Heil our new Fuehrer, Ernie's pud.'!"

So that is how it came to be
That our young lad missed Wigan tea,
But did he care? My goodness, no!
'Cos he'd dropped pud. on old So-and-so!

55

56

Musso the Wop; Beano; May 1941; (Artie Jackson); © D.C. Thomson.

Musso the Wop; Beano; October 1941; (Artie Jackson); © D.C. Thomson.

Musso the Wop; Beano; August 1942; (Artist Unknown); © D.C. Thomson.

Our Ernie; Knock-Out; January 1943; (A.J. Kelly); © Amalgamated Press.

OUR ERNIE
MRS. ENTWHISTLE'S LITTLE LAD.

Right in the middle of morning class,
Ernie cried, "Achtung! Let me pass!
Heinkel! Heil Tickler! Get out of my way!
I'm goose-stepping home to-day!"

Schoolmaster, doing song and dance,
Yelled, " Ee, I'd like to dust your pants!
I don't lose temper as a'rule,
But, by gum, you're disgrace to my school."

So off, goose-stepping, went our lad,
And folks in Wigan got quite mad.
A bobby cried, "I'll tell my serge of you!"
And little nipper shouted "Boo!"

At home Ma said to little Sis,
"Switch on, lass, we don't want to miss
The news on our new radio set—
It's better now than we used to get."

But in marched Ernie, looking stern,
And gave the radio knobs a turn,
Till he got Bremensender on the air,
And tho' his pa were wild he didn't care.

Cried pa, "Tha's gone out of thy mind,"
As lad tore hole in black-out blind,
And warden called to give them warning,
They might be summoned in the morning.

Then lad went out and soon reached door,
Of local War Department store,
And to the key-hole placed an eye,
Like Funf— well-known fifth column spy.

But Home Guard sentry watched him do it,
And pounced on lad before he knew it,
And officer cried, "Ee, you did that well,
Take prisoner and bung him in a cell!"

Next morning, prompt at nine o'clock,
Our lad were standing in the dock,
And judge said it were plain to see
He'd broken Rule 961,123.

The judge blew nose and drew a breff,
And said, "The sentence, lad, is deff!"
But ma came begging mercy for her lad,
Who'd always been good—when he weren't bad.

They called a doctor then to see
If he could solve the mystery
Of what had happened to the lad,
To make him nasti, queer and bad.

Well, it turned out just like Ma thought—
'Twere German Measles lad had caught,
So to bed he went and when he were undressed
They found Swash-ticklers on his chest.

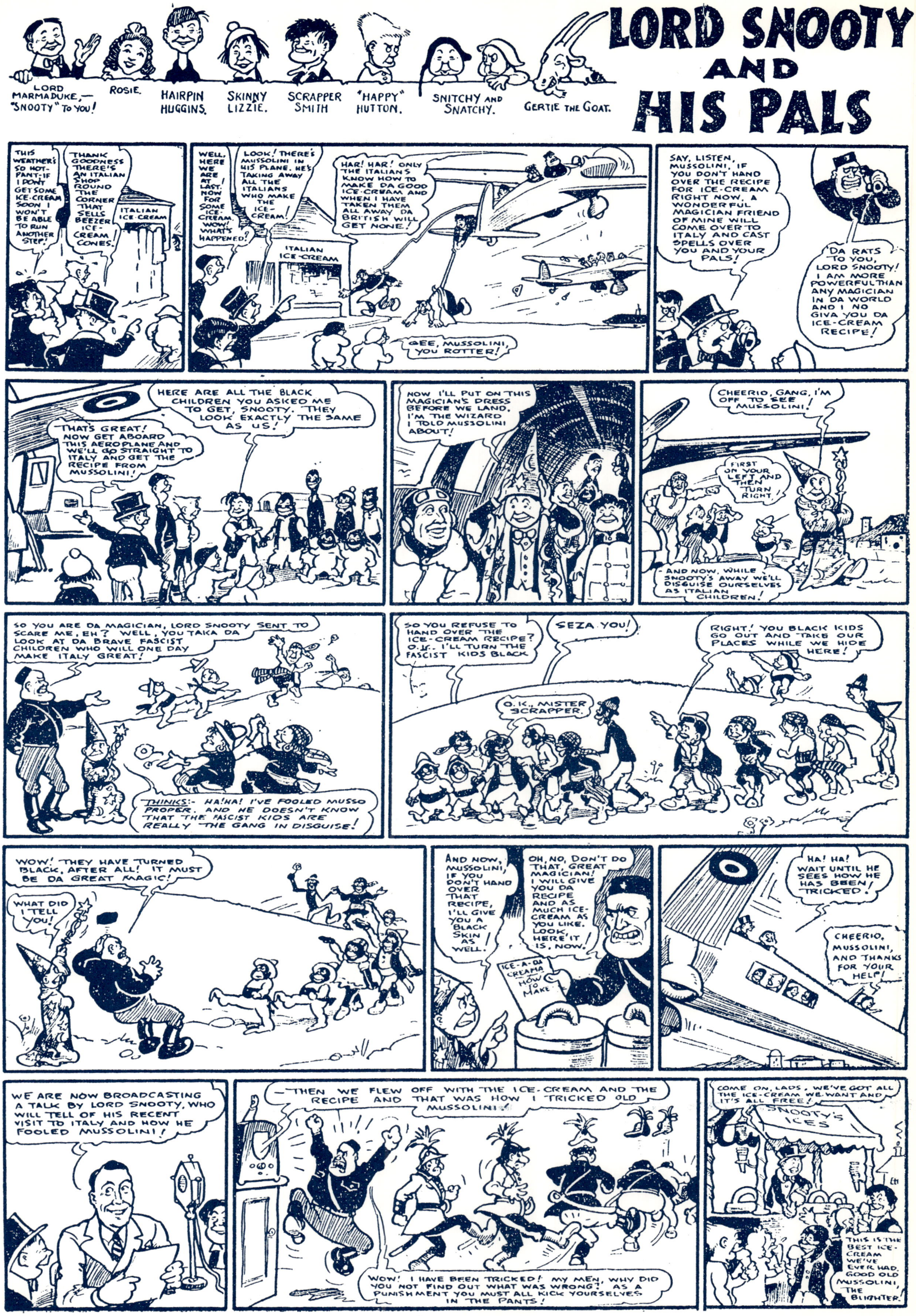

Lord Snooty; Beano; August 1940; (Dudley Watkins); © D.C. Thomson.

DOING THEIR BIT!

STARS IN BATTLEDRESS!

The most curious call-up of the war occurred on May 25th, 1940. It was on this day that readers of **Film Fun** discovered that virtually all of that comic's all-star bill had joined the army! Spectacles proved no obstacle to Harold Lloyd, it seemed, nor did his American nationality. He was a private soldier, just like Joe E. Brown, Laurel and Hardy, Lupino Lane and Claude Hulbert! And one week later, Old Mother Riley and her Daughter Kitty, as enacted by Arthur Lucan and Kitty McShane, were having a go at the food hoarders.

Across the other side of the media in **Radio Fun,** home front ho-ho was the order of the day. Big-Hearted Arthur Askey and his pal, Richard 'Stinker' Murdoch, were building their government-issue Anderson Shelters in the back yard, while Bud Flanagan and Chesney Allan joined the A.R.P., Tommy Handley the **I.T.M.A.** star, put the weekly wind up his radio opponent, Funf the German Spy. For the rest of show business it was tin-hats, gas-masks, blackouts and the Black Market.

Arthur Askey; Radio Fun; November 1939; (Reg Parlett); © Amalgamated Press.

Charlie Chaplin; Funny Wonder; October 1939; (Bertie Brown); © Amalgamated Press.

Jack Warner; Radio Fun; December 1941; (John Jukes); © Amalgamated Press.

JACK (MIND MY BIKE) WARNER
AND HIS LITTEL GEL, JOAN WINTERS

1. Dear Boys and "Gels,"—The other morning Colonel Cornplaster sent for me and my "littel gel" and told us that we were to go on the air that evening. "That gives me a ril frill, sir," I said. "Oh rather," chipped in Joan Winters. Then I hopped on my bike and set off down to the village to get the script. I didn't know that Sergeant Sossidgeskin was doing a nice quiet lurk round the corner with a brick—waiting for littel me—de-dah, de-dah. And the old maggot chucked that piece of wall down in front of my jolly old bike. "That'll 'alt 'im!" snarled Sergy.

2. "Ha—you two-faced old twicer!" I sniggered. "I've missed it, see!" "'Sright—you 'ave, but you hain't missed that tree, hold Clever Dick," roared Sergy, as in missing the brick I ran slap bang into a young tree. But that tree was a nice bender, and so I just ran up and over it and when it sprang up it copped Sergy a clout across the countenance. I thought I'd seen the last of him then, but the old nit-wit followed me.

3. And while I was having a chinwag with and collecting the script from Alvar Dongfrage, old Sossidgeskin tied a squeaker on my back tyre which made me think the old bike wanted a spot of oil. So I borrowed a squirtful from the garage and treated the back bearings to a bath. Some of that oil spread itself on the road, too, just as Sergy trundled by on his bike. "If he gets on that nice little drop of oil—oh de-dah, de-dah!" I trilled.

4. Sergy got on to that slippery patch just like as if I'd told him to and then he went right into a dizzy whizz. "You always were a ril good turn, Sergy," I said. "But you didn't oughter a done it." I left him to his skiddy larks and tootled on to Garrison Theatre to do my turn with my "littel gel." And was I good—I mean were we good? Well, you oughter know!

Jack Warner

63

FLANAGAN AND ALLEN
Oi! Up to Their Fun Again! Oi!

1. Bud Flanagan and Chesney Allen joined the A.R.P, last Thirstday—sorry, we mean Thursday! They were given the job of filling sandbags. "Get busy, Bud!" said Ches. "We've got to finish this!" So Bud put a hard-working look on his face.

2. Ches started work, but Bud was suffering from housemaid's elbow. "I darling!" he cried suddenly. Ches looked round. "What do you mean—'I darling'?" he asked. "I 'dear'!" answered Bud. "Oi! I've just got a bright notion!" He put a bone in the sand and told a near-by tripe-hound to fetch it!

3. The dog didn't need telling twice to go and fetch the bone, and as it scratched away at the sand, Bud's sandbags got filled in less time than it takes a kipper to shake its fin. "My brain-wave is certainly coming up to 'scratch'!" chuckled Bud, joyfully.

4. A few ticks later, Bud had finished filling all his sandbags and reported to Ches for more. Chesney Allen nearly had three pink fits with blue trimmings. "Can I have some more grit-covers?" asked Bud. "Grit-covers?" cried Ches, wrinkling his brow. "You mean sandbags! Oi!"

5. Our comical coconibs decided they'd done enough sandbagging for a while, so they trotted off to pastures new. Suddenly they caught sight of a poster warning people to keep a look-out for foreign spies, and report anything suspicious.

6. Ches began to get very red in the face. "I wish I could find a mean spy!" he cried, clenching his fists. "If only I could lay my hands on one!" Bud offered to produce one for the small sum of two copper coins.

7. Back came Bud and in his hand was a mince-pie. "Bah! You feather-brained nitwit! I said 'mean spy,'—not mince-pie!" yelled Ches. "Very well," answered Bud. "If you don't want it, I'll eat it, see?"

Flanagan and Allen; Radio Fun; November 1939; (Alex Akerbladh); © Amalgamated Press.

8. Ambling onwards our pals suddenly heard something which sounded so suspicious, they nearly fell over each other's corns, trying to get an earful of hark. They heard two sinister-looking gents with long trimmings arranging to meet with some plans at the Red Barn on the common at 8 p.m.

9. Shortly afterwards, Ches and Bud heard something else which nearly made them jump out of their boots. High up in an old building, they saw two more sinister figures and once again the men were talking about plans and the Red Barn on Rose Common. Oo-er!

10. "I don't need to be Inspector Stanley to know that those men are spies!" muttered Chesney Allen in a deep voice about three feet wide. Bud offered to go to the police but Ches brushed him aside. "I'm going to take charge of this matter personally!" he exclaimed.

11. Ches dashed round to the drill-hall of the 19th Royal Outsiders. "I want all of you, lads!" he cried. "I've just heard something of the gravest national importance. I've found some spies at work!" The soldiers packed up their troubles in their old kitbags and followed!

12. Having called out the Army, Ches called out the Women's Auxiliary Territorials, the Women's Land Army, and any more to come, glad of it! "I am in charge of the great round-up, ladies!" he coughed.

13. Ches Allen soon began to feel very important! Having told the Army, Navy, Air Force, Firemen, and Ambulance Drivers all about the meeting of the spies in the old Red Barn, he began to lead the procession towards Rose Common. The whole business required such secrecy, they all started to say "Shush!" and the noise echoed over the countryside for miles!

14. A rude shock awaited poor old Ches, however! Arriving at the Red Barn, they pushed open the door and were just in time to hear the Mayor open the town council meeting to discuss the plans of the new sewer. Poor old Ches, had made a slight mistook, we thinks!

15. The Army, Navy, and Air Force made their way home—and Ches Allen was at the front! "The war's really started!" said Bud, as the men began to tell Ches what they thought of him. "He was only trying to execute his piece!" "Do his bit!" corrected Winnie. "Oi!"

65

Haver and Lee; Radio Fun; March 1942; (Alex Akerbladh); © Amalgamated Press.

HAVER AND LEE
THE VERY PRIVATE DETECTIVES
DUCKWEED — EGGBLOW

1. What a spooky task Haver and Lee, the world-wide famous 'tecs, take on this week! You can see by one glimpse at per above that Lord Moneybags is hiring the tame sleuths to lay the ghost by the heels or otherwise do away with the rummy goings-on! Not a nice job to take on, but Duckweed and Eggblow fear nothing and nobody—except the rent man. They wish that Goofy the Ghost was around to help them—he'd soon do away with the spooks if they weren't in the Ghosts' Union! Hey, what's this going on behind our 'tecs? Gig-gosh! It's a spook in full flight!

2. Well, look at that! The spook on the flying trapeze has given old Duckweed a bootful of kick and an earful of wham! And what's this the spook is up to now? Well, bless my soap ration, he's lapped up Eggblow and there they go swinging right up on to the balcony! Poor Eggy hasn't got a "ghost" of a chance of getting away! Meanwhile, Duckweed's all of a dither. Golly, now two hands appear and collar him, too!

3. My, what a haunted mansion this is! One minute the 'tecs are there, next minute they are on the missing list! Hey, whoa back, here's Duckweed popping up in the picture again. That pair of five fingers dirtying Duckweed's collar belong to Jim Kneesweep, one of a black market gang! Yoiks, here's old Eggy turned up like a bad penny, and see, it isn't a real ghost that's got him after all. It's a bad lad with his mum's sheet!

4. The imitation ghostie gives Eggy such a fourpen'orth of shove that our comical coughdrop cannons into all the tins of lovely grub and the three bad ones feel the force of their own black market! Ha, ha, serves them right! Our tame sleuths are still in one piece and alive and kicking, so down the chute they shoot the black marketeers! There they go! Lord Moneybags hands over a nice fat fee to the lads for laying the ghosties!

The Western Brothers; Radio Fun; April 1942; (George Heath); © Amalgamated Press.

The WESTERN BROTHERS
PLAY THE GAME, YOU CADS!

1. Kenneth and George Western are going to give us an eyeful of some real, honest-to-goodness Home Guard tactics. The local H.G.s are going to do a drop of attacking, but first of all the cads are told they must get into Little Twittering by fair means, or in the dark, and do a spot of spying. Ver-ree difficult! But not for Ken and George. They disguise themselves as the spare parts of a dance band, play "Friend o' Mine" very soothingly to the sentry and—whoops dearie!—here they are in the town, which they subject to a "full scale" attack with their melody makers.

2. Oh—this is good, this is. The grocer, who doesn't like their music and chucks a bag of flour at them, nearly gets his own back. Instead, the flour bag hits the O.C. in charge of the Home Guards defending the town in the ear. Of course, he doesn't like it, and before he can flash his old school tie Kenneth is cast into clink, to the great grief of brother George. But what's George doing about it? He can't let his college chum down!

3. Don't worry, folks—already a plan has boiled up in George's brain pan. What is it? Why, he just fixes a file on the end of his trombone, tears off a few nice bars of "Home Sweet Home," and cuts through the bars of Kenneth's new "Home, Not-so-sweet Home." Good-ho! Ken's free. Nice work, George! Now what? Well, they have got another couple of sentries to get past. Quiet, please—Kenneth is doing a deep think.

4. Ha, ha! He's got a piping hot wheeze this time, readers, and the two sentries poke their noses right into it. My word—they're nicely coupled up by their scent detectors, aren't they, and while they're having a bit of an argument about it George and Kenneth let in their own Home Guard team, who take Little Twittering in about two twitches of a tadpole's tailpiece. Well played, cads—you deserve a medal. That's what the sergeant thinks, too, for he invests the heroes with the G.N.O.O.S.T.—Grand and Noble Order of the Old School Tie! Hooray! Win 'em and wear 'em, cads!

Arthur Askey; Radio Fun; November 1939; (Reg Parlett); © Amalgamated Press.

Sandy Powell; Radio Fun; November 1939; (George Parlett); © Amalgamated Press.

SANDY POWELL

SANDY POWELL REALLY BRINGS THE HOUSE DOWN THIS WEEK! But life isn't so black as it's painted after all! Laugh with your old "Powell" Sandy to-day!

1. Good mornin', lads and lasses! Ee, I had a brainwave, t' other day. I thowt I'd "dazzle-paint" house so that bombin' planes would think nowt was there!

2. I went straight into shop, and asked for dazzle-paint but yon shopkeeper hadn't any in stock! By goom, I felt a bit worried then, I can tell thee, chums!

3. So out I went, hopin' that Hitler would refrain from fireworks till house was camouflaged! I didn't notice crook o' me stick had caught in a pot o' paint!

4. Ay, but I did soon! Weight of pot sent stick clean up in me face with a bang!

5. While I was rubbin' me injured snitch, I discovered I'd managed to hook t' paint!

6. Ee, I dashed across street like a fairy. "Now to paint house," I cried.

7. Well, I made a reet good job o' same, but Mr. Noel Knowall laughed at me an' told me t' idea was daft. "You can see it a mile off!" he cried.

8. "Tha' can't, I bet thee!" I retorted, sharp-like but cool. "Come across road, and see it for thyself." So away we went.

9. Well, I thowt as how house looked like a bit o' open country, but old Knowall said it stood out as plain as t' nose on me face!

10. But just then, up rolled a steam-roller who mistook my lovely house for a short cut! Meanwhile, old Knowall was tellin' me how much safer his house was without paint.

11. Ee, what a crash it was when steam-roller went through house! I thowt old Knowall 'ud never stop laughin'!

12. What a surprise when he found I'd painted his house by mistake an' steam-roller 'had demolished same! Bye-bye!

69

OLD MOTHER RILEY featuring LUCAN & McSHANE

FILM FUN — JUN. 1 1940.

1. Folks, meet Old Mother Riley! Of course, you must have seen her many times on the films and laughed at her very funny adventures. Well, now you have the chance to laugh at them in FILM FUN. But she had nothing to laugh about the other not-so-fine day when she found that the cupboard was brim full to the very top with NOTHING! It seemed that nothing but the workhouse was staring her in the face unless she went out and looked for work.

2. "You can't keep a good man down," said the diver, as he came up for air, and we say you can't keep Old Mother Riley down, either. No, she has a habit of bobbing up when least expected. Her fairy-like feet—quite a large fairy—took her round corners and round squares, and eventually she paused for a breather outside Professor Skinner's Slimming Institute. A charlady was wanted, and the dear old duck meant to rub her fingers to the bone to earn cash.

3. Professor Skinner was so thin that when he turned sideways he could have been marked absent. He looked as crusty as an over-baked cottage loaf, too. But this did not worry Old Mother Riley. For she clicked for the job. Prof. Skinner—should have been Skinny—told her that she could start right away, if not before. Her job was as easy as eating peas with a knife. All she had to do was to make a clean sweep of things, and show gents into his office.

4. Old Mother Riley has put in some good work with a dustpan and broom in her time, and as she had had plenty of practice the job of sweeping up did not come at all strange to her. The job was not so dusty after all, she told herself, even if the hall was. She was going about her duties, trying to make herself look busy when in trooped a trio of gents who looked as if they did nothing else but eat. They looked as if they could do with some slimming.

5. The leading gent was about sixty-five inches round the old rumtum, and if he had been approaching round a corner you would have seen him coming a full minute before his face appeared. But when he toddled out of Professor Skinner's office ten minutes later he seemed a mere shadow of his former self. All his plumpness had disappeared as if by magic. Old Mother Riley was naturally very surpruzzled, and small wonder. She could not "figure" it out at all.

6. Our old duchess told herself that if she ever got as fat as that chap had been, which she hoped she wouldn't, she would call on Skinner herself. Her thoughts were soon interrupted, however. A stout fellow who looked very broad round the beam, wherever that is, trotted into the prems. If the other chap had been fat—well, he was a veritable mountain. He seemed bulging with his own self-importance, and as bold as brass, inquired for the prof.

Old Mother Riley; Film Fun; June 1940; (Norman Ward); © Amalgamated Press.

7. Old Mother Riley remembered, without having a reminder, that she had been told to direct paying clients and ready-money customers into Skinner's office, and she did as ordered. To make certain that she made no mistook she raised her broom, and pointed it towards the door. The handle gave the fat gent a rough handling.

8. It became mixed up with his large coat, the buttons came undone, and he was undone, so to speak. Because he wasn't a fat chap at all. No, we're not kidding. His coat was an outsize one, admitted, but he had no rumtum of which to boast. His coat was stuffed with food, and when it fell open the good grub fell to the floor.

9. He felt properly shown up, and realising he had been exposed, made for the door at high speed. He vanished through the aperture which the door usually filled when closed, and left Old Mother Riley to her thoughts. Now as you know, she is a cute old dear, and it did not take her a month of Mondays to realise something was up.

10. That food gave her food for thought, and she came to the conclusion a spot of investigating in the old Jack Keen style would not do any harm. As silently as a mouse stepping noiselessly on a thick pile Persian carpet, she opened the door. Inside things were going on. It was as plain as Skinner's face that he was a food hoarder.

11. Old Mother Riley called in a limb of the law, P.-c. Porridge, and together they made their way downstairs where the kitchen nuts were kept. Our dear old thing then put in some nifty work with a saw, for it was obvious to anyone with a couple of ears that the dirty work was proceeding just above them. Chest a minute, folks.

12. You will soon have inside information as to what was in that chest. Yes, it was full to the brim with foodery, as Old Mother Riley revealed when she sawed through the boards. Unknown to those above she removed the bottom, and that chest, like Old Mother Riley's cupboard and old Mother Hubbard's cupboard, was bare.

13. Then the bobbie bobbed up. Porridge was a man of action when he got going, and he darted up through the bottom of the chest. He whipped open the lid, to observe Professor Skinner with more eats. It was a fair cop, and Skinner, the nasty food hoarder, was caught in the very act. And all the praise, and lots of it was going, was due to none other than our dear Old Mother Riley.

14. Praise was not the only thing she received, however. No, for rounding up the food hoarder she received a spot of the proceeds, a ham, tongue, butter, etc., etc., and etc. What was more she was given a fiver for luck, and she found it all very acceptable. She toddled back to her old homestead, and Kitty said a mouthful when she saw all the choice eats. Now let's leave them to it.

"A.K. 1313"! GRAND NEW SERIAL ON PAGE 7.

Film Fun 2d

No. 1,062.   Every Tuesday.   May 25th, 1940.

LAUREL & HARDY in
Their Latest Film "The Flying Deuces"

This Week: PROPERLY IN THE CART!

Hallo, Folks. — It seems that our lucky lads don't appear to be doing too well in the jolly old Army, and it wouldn't surprise me a little bit if Sergeant Strafem gets a bit out of temper with them before long, and that he will fall out with them.

Panel 1 speech: "If it's not a rude question, Private Hardy, what are you supposed to be doing?" "I heard somebody shout 'Fall in!' so I fell in." "And I was just going to fall in too, sir!"

2. Well, folks, I think you will agree with me that Olly made a perfect twirp of himself by falling into the horse-trough, and Stan didn't do much better, either. It wasn't very long before Strafem discovered that in Stan and Olly he had a couple of prize idiots.

Panel speech: "And look at you! Can't you smarten yourself up? Don't you know you're wearing the King's uniform?" "I thought it was a bit too big for me, Sarge!"

3. It was as plain as mud to the sergeant that the sooner he got rid of the new recruits the better. Olly tried to get into his good books by addressing him as sergeant-major, but even this failed to work the oracle. Up trooped a jolly old C.O. with an important dispatch.

Panel speech: "When I see men like you it makes me feel I want to lie down and cry. I've got to shift you fellows at an early date." "I don't think the Sergeant Major likes us very much, Stan." "That's just what I was thinking, Olly." "I want two good men to take an important dispatch for me."

4. Sergeant Strafem was an artful card, and he realised that if he recommended Stan and Olly to carry the message he would get rid of them for a long period. So let us go with the boys and see General Chutney at Cayenne Barracks to see how they get on with the job.

Panel speech: "I recommend these men, sir, if you want the dispatch taken a long distance." "Take this to General Chutney at Cayenne Barracks. This is an important dispatch and MUST be delivered WITHOUT FAIL."

5. It was a long walk to Cayenne Barracks, and the boys decided to borrow a tandem. They started off in style, whilst the sergeant chuckled up his left cuff with great joy at having got rid of them. Our lads were delighted they'd been entrusted with the special message.

Panel speech: "Roll out the barrel — we'll have a barrel of fun." "It's a good thing for those chaps they've gone. It was a smart idea of mine to get rid of those cissies."

6. As you know, Olly's no light weight, and it wasn't surprising that when the front wheel of the tandem hit a boulder the boulder won. "You remember what the C.O. said!" cried Olly. "We must deliver this dispatch without fail. We must borrow that cart, whether the chap who owns it likes it or not." So they jolly well borrowed it!

Panel speech: "That's caused it, Olly! Another fine mess we've got ourselves into." "You must commandeer that handcart, Stan."

7. As usual, the boys pushed all before them and, having placed the tandem in the cart, they toddled along in grand style. It was hard work pushing that barrow up hill and down dale and down hill and up dale, but they seemed to be getting along all right now. It was most decidedly a case of push and go. *(Continued on page 24.)*

Panel speech: "I'll bet we get promoted when the General sees us!" "If you want to get on in the Army, Stan, you must have plenty of push and carry everything before you — just as we're doing."

72

Laurel and Hardy; Film Fun; May 1940; (Billy Wakefield); © Amalgamated Press.

FILM FUN — 21 — MAY 25, 1940.

8. Bad luck seems to be lurking around every corner, and another bit of bad luck buckled the wheel of the barrow. In the circs, they discovered that they could not proceed any farther. It was then that Olly's eagle optic alighted upon the farmer's cart, complete with jolly old horse and harness. "We'll borrow the cart!" said Olly.

9. They told the farmer where to get off, borrowed the cart, placed the barrow and bike inside, and seated themselves as comfortably as possible. "We've just got to get this dispatch to Cayenne Barracks," said Olly. "It must be delivered without fail." Stan felt sorry the poor horse had to do all the donkey work, and said so to his old pal.

10. Then the old nag put on the four-wheel brakes and refused to budge. Olly realised that something would have to be done, and when he saw a car coming along he decided to commandeer it at the earliest possible moment, if not before. That dispatch had got to be taken to Cayenne Barracks without fail, and that was surely that.

11. Then the car, complete with horse and cart, barrow and tandem, not to mention Stan and Olly, proceeded on its way, with Olly taking the front seat, as usual. Now it looks as if everything is plain sailing and that they will reach the barracks in good time. I have a feeling, however, that something is going to happen.

12. What did I tell you? The car's broken down now! It certainly put a full stop to their progress, but Olly wasn't going to be done. He remembered the words of the jolly old C.O.—that the dispatch must be delivered without fail. That was why he decided to borrow the lorry, even if the driver chappie wouldn't give him permission.

13. Well, here they are arriving. They certainly got there all right, after a tremendous amount of trouble. The troops got a bit of a shock when they saw Stan and Olly sitting in the barrow, which was in the cart, which was in the car, which was in the lorry. Everything looks as if it's going to turn out fine for our lads, doesn't it?

14. When General Chutney saw our boys and Olly handed over the dispatch to him even the rain couldn't damp his enthusiasm. He told the boys exactly what he thought of them, and said they were a couple of brave lads. It looks as if our couple of coughdrops are going to finish up this week in real grand style. They thought they'd get a couple of putty medals with knobs on and all the latest improvements, and that they'd be promoted. Judging by what the old colonel is saying, that's just what's going to happen to them, and they had every reason to think so. The rain came pouring down, severely wetting our lads. Neither of them dreamed what was going to happen.

15. Just fancy! Olly and Stan had dreamed it all, and when they woke up they found they were getting wet because the ceiling was leaking. And so that ends that little episode! But next week the boys come off very well indeed, you'll be glad to learn, and I hope you will order your copy in advance so that you'll be sure to get FILM FUN. You must not miss next week's adventure, which is entitled: "All at Sea!" Cheerio, folks, until then, when I shall have the pleasure of being with you once again.—Yours very merrily,

Eddie, The Happy Editor

THAT POPULAR FILM STAR "OLD MOTHER RILEY" POSITIVELY APPEARS NEXT WEEK!

Claude Hulbert; Film Fun; May 1940; (Tom Radford); © Amalgamated Press.

Meet THE MERRIEST of MOVIELANDS MIRTH MAKERS
Claude Hulbert

Panel 1: "What about that ten bob you owe me Claude?" / "Sorry, I'm a bit short this week!" / "I'll see you have it soon old pal!" / "Yes do, the sooner the quicker!" / "I'll bet he's just drawn his pay!" / "I don't like the look of him!"

1. Dear old Claude always makes a rule never to borrow money, but as he did not want his cash to be alone, he had a loan of ten bob. The chap whom he borrowed the dough from went under the name of Cadger, and as a matter of fact he was a proper cadger. He was not a nice chap to know once you knew him, and Claude soon found this out. Cadger was out to get that ten bob back at the earliest possible moment, his idea being to then touch Claude for a bit, and pay him back ten years later. But Claude said he could not spare it that week.

Panel 2: "Hoi! Hand over yer money buddy!" / "I'm off!" / "Here's the ten bob I owed you. Now we're all square. I'm in a hurry." / "Okay thanks!" / "You'll do just as well! Hand over all yer money!" / "I got out of that well!"

2. Directly our cheery one left Cadger he ran into a spot of trouble. One of the filching fraternity was in the near vicinity, and he had something to say. He wanted Claude's money, and he meant to have it by hook or by crook—preferably by crook. He chased after Claude, who showed him a clean pair of Army boots for a while. But our chum who had done a twelve-mile route march that day realised that he could not run much farther, so spotting Cadger he thought of a really clever notion. He handed him back the ten boblets which he owed him.

Panel 3: "Why were you in such a hurry to pay me that ten bob?" / "Why if he had got the money off me—I should still have owed you the 10/-!" / "Gee! I'm 10 minutes late on pass! I'll get over the wall!" / "That's done it! Look at the spikes!"

3. The result was that Cadger fell for it, for the tough made him pass over all his spare cash. Cadger could not see through our lad's little lark and asked why he had been in such a terrific hurry to repay him the money. Claude told him the truth, of course. Well, having put paid to Cadger, Claude went off to music practice. He arrived back at barracks ten minutes late by his watch, and he knew that he would be for it if he were spotted. He would have got over the wall, but the spikes on top did not suggest that this would be easy.

Panel 4: "My flute! Good thing I had it with me!" / "Over the top with the best of luck!" / "Goodnight everybody. G——ood n——ight!"

4. This would have barred the way to any ordinary person, but we all know our cheery one is possessed of a brain far in advance of the average. The tin whistle on which he had been blowing during music practice came in very handy, for the stops on it dropped over the spikes. The result was that good old Claude was able to rise to great heights, and if you want some inside information, he got into the barracks undetected. It was a very clever notion, if we may so say, and we do not hesitate to say it. Claude crept into his bunk and no one was any the wiser that he had arrived late home. And as he now wants to go to sleep we will leave him until next week at the same time.

DUGGIE WAKEFIELD

DUGGIE PUTS THE TIN HAT ON IT THIS WEEK! "Be prepared" is our Lancashire Lad's motto, and he's determined to play "bombs-a-daisy" with his brainbox well covered! This way for laughs!

1. Mornin' all! T' other day I had fierce argument with Sam Snooper. T' gormless goomph said A.R.P. were all a lot o' piffle!

2. Then a lot o' black shapes appeared in the sky. "Wow! Bombers!" I yelled, doing swallow-dive into nearest air-raid shelter. Sam stood where he were, and just laughed! S' fact!

3. But he didn't laugh for long! As ducks flew over he tried to duck, but fell with hearty splosh in t' nearby duck pond. Ee, I did chuckle!

4. "'Water' state you're in, lad," I said, emerging from air-raid shelter. "Serves you right for givin' me t' bird!" Ee, he were wet!

5. On t' way home we passed shop where they were sellin' tin hats. "Ee, I'll treat me old brainbox to one o' those!" I said.

6. "I'll have this one!" I chortled, choosing hat me own size at bottom o' pile. "Tee hee," sniggered Sam. "You're daft, lad. Nothing will fall on us!"

7. By goom, he were wrong there! I thought t' were town hall clock striking, but t' were tin hats clonking on Sam's top-knot!

8. We both had a "fit" at t' same time! As I tried on me new headgear, Sam decided he'd be safer in t' air raid shelter.

9. But noises from dug-out sounded as though Sam were havin' air raid all to himself. "What's happenin'?" I wondered.

10. Next minute Sam came shootin' out like shell from gun. He'd interrupted wardens' game o' darts, and they'd sent him out at t' "double"! "Warden" nice to-do!

11. Poor old Sam had A Reet Proper do wi' A.R.P.! But how do you like me new headgear? Bye-bye all!

JOE E. BROWN
The Famous Fellow of The Films

Our Big Noise Speaks up for Himself This Week

This Week: STOUT FELLOWS!

1. Howdy, Folks.—The recruiting sergeant stopped me the other day and told me that if I wanted to say a few words in favour of the Army I could go out on recruiting patrol. I said that that would suit me down to the ground, and I promised not to go into the milk bar to have one, but to give my whole attention to the job in hand.

2. It is not easy to find recruits when you are out looking for them, however. They are few and far between like lobsters in a lobster sandwich. One old gent about ninety in the shade and ninety-one in the sun did volunteer, but I told him to wait until he was older.

3. I soon realised that the old Joe Brown brainpan would have to concoct some smart idea. No sooner said than done. I painted a notice on the wall: "To fat men only," and then wrote something in small print so they would have to get very close to the advert.

4. My plan shaped according to plan. Along came a very fat gent, and spotting the notice he thought that as his girth was a bit swell he came under the category of a fat man. As a matter of fact, he was so fat that if he had laid down in the road and rolled over he would have rocked himself to sleep. He read the notice I had left.

5. Now, when he read the notice, his white waistcoat had pressed against the notice written back to front underneath. So that when he moved away a notice could be seen displayed on his waistcoat. It read: "Join the Army and see the world." Of course, the fat chap, not being able to see his toes, was also unaware of the notice.

6. Two of his fat pals, making three stout fellows in all, came along to read the notice, and on their white waistcoats the notices were plain to see, if anyone happened to look that way. The prospect of seeing the world evidently appealed to the lads of that village, for one and all and a few others agreed that it would be a good thing for them if they joined the Army there and then without any delay.

7. The recruits rolled in one by one and in their crowds, and when I reported back to barracks I came in for a large spot of applause from the recruiting sergeant. He said that I was a proper lad and that he would recommend me to himself for promotion. He accepted his own recommendation there and then and told me that I was promoted to the cookhouse. Very doubtful promotion, eh?

Joe E. Brown; Film Fun; May 1940; (Tom Radford); © Amalgamated Press.

8. Still, who was I to quibble? Not me. The corporal—the lad with two stripes—in charge of the cookhouse, told me to take some doughnuts over to the sergeants' mess. As I was there to obey orders, and a corporal must be obeyed, I said that it would be done. They looked juicy, did those doughnuts, and very fruity, too.

9. They smelt so good that if I had not have been on my best behaviour and in the Army I could have easily eaten the whole plateful. They made my mouth water and I longed to sink my molars into them, but being an honest sort of chap I realised things like that were not done. But some other things were being done.

10. A couple of pals of mine—you would not have thought so—decided to play a joke on me whilst my back was turned. To get to the sergeants' mess, I had to cross a field, and in the neighbouring field a playful bull lived. Now, separating these two fields was a gate which remained closed except when open, and the two tommies opened it. The playful bull saw a chance to get playful and chased me.

11. Bulls are amiable creatures until they get put-out, but they always seem to be put-out when I meet them. This one evidently did not like the look of my dial and chased me at the double. As I could not move quite so fast as this with my Army boots on, I realised that something would have to be done. I had heard of that saying of taking the bull by the horns, but did not think it much good trying.

12. Those sharp horns looked very sharp indeed, and I did not fancy having them introduced to the seat of my pants. It was for this reason that I decided to try to soften the blow. I still had the doughnuts with me, and one by one and one at a time I placed them on the bull's prodders. He did not have anything to say about it, but wanted to make a hit with me more than ever.

13. You know, if it was not for my jolly old brain working that one out, it would be a toss up whether I would have been out of hospital to tell you this tale. But when the bull did catch me, I did not catch it. No, quite the contradict. The doughnuts softened the blow, so to speak, and I must admit, without considering that I am boasting that I rose to the occasion on that occasion.

14. I flew through the air with the greatest of ease and a large spot of speed and landed in the sergeants' mess the other side of a nice kind fence. I was now out of the danger zone and the doughnuts had caused me to think that someone had struck me a fierce one with a sackful of feathers. Now all that remained to be didst was to deliver the doughnuts. Luckily, the bull did not return to its own private field with the doughnuts, but just stood there with a nasty look in its optic, hoping that I would return whence I had come. So I was able to take the doughnuts from its prodders much to the pleasure of the C.O., who was having a chat with the dear sergeants.

15. He said that as I was so intrepid, brave, and not to mention fearless, and a clever, intelligent, and brainy chap into the bargain, he duly considered after a great deal of thought, that I was entitled to be promoted. He made me a fully-blown sergeant. Next week—ah, I must not give the game away—I will be back again in a side-splitter which is entitled: "A Black Outlook." Do not miss this treat, folks!

*Laughingly yours,
Joe E. Brown*

Lupino Lane; Film Fun; May 1940; (Tom Radford); © Amalgamated Press.

FUN IN THE LAMBETH WALK
Lupino Lane

1. Things were moving in the Army—they usually do, except when they are at a standstill—and Bill was informed by the sarg that he was due to attend for physical jerks. Bill realised that he would have to put a jerk in it and get into line, and here we see him with the rest. The order was to "Touch Your Toes," and the thing to do in the circs was to keep the legs straight and do the necessary with fingers. But Bill thought differently. With a swift movement he took off his shoes and followed suit with his nice new Army socks.

2. Of course, the sarg did not know what was what or what was happening, and he had a few words to say on the matter. In a voice which sounded like the bellowing of a ferocious bull, he demanded to know what was what and why. Bill explained in a sentence, which, although short, was straight to the point. He said that it was absolutely imposs to touch his toes whilst his boots were on, so he had taken them off. This took the wind out of the sarg's sails so much that he could not find words to cope with the situation. So he dismissed the squad.

3. Later—we don't know how much later—Bill was walking along thinking of nothing in partick when he heard that voice he disliked so much. It was the sarg and he had a few words to say about our lad's personal appearance. Very rude, don't you think? We think so, too. But there was nothing our cheery one could say about it, so he said nothing. The sarg told him that his putty was undone, and that he was to do it up immediately if not before. Bill, who does not stoop to anything so low as a rule, had to comply with the sarg's order.

4. One thing he overlooked, or did not see, however. That was as he did the putty up he tied it to the leg of the seat on which the sarg was reclining. This was rather upsetting. Yes, for when the bullying chappie told our chum to step on it, Bill rather put his foot in it, so to speak. For when he stepped it out as ordered, the sergeant fell all of a heap. You see, the putty tugged the seat over and the sarg bit the dust. Serve him right, too, if we may say so, which we may—having given ourselves permiss. Well, Bill realised then that he had better apply for leave before he was given seven days or maybe a week C.B. So he hopped it at the jolly old double.

Harold Lloyd; Film Fun; May 1940; (Norman Ward); © Amalgamated Press.

HAROLD LLOYD
THE FUNNY MAN OF THE FILMS

1. T'other day Harold was called to the officer's office and ordered to take the pass for that night to the colonel as quickly as poss. One has to do what one's told when one's in the Army, so Harold took the paper, and said okey-doke, or words to that effect. Our pal must have been listening to the h'officer with one ear, 'cos he thought the Big Pot said "pass word." Anyoldhow, he passed out of the office, and, as luck would have it, the bugler was blowing on his bugle just outside. He blew the paper out of Harold's mitt.

2. This put the wind up Harold, and he dashed after the paper, but, unforch, it got caught on the barbed wire. "What a blow!" gasped our pal. "I'll have to get it somehow." The next see he scrambled over the wire and retrieved the paper, and, needless to say, this little lark didn't improve his battle dress. No, it looked very much the worse for wear, but this didn't get Harold's rag out. He tore off in the way he should go, and when he reached the cookhouse he espied the dispatch rider. He decided to get a lift in the side car.

3. As the dispatch rider started up his engine Harold took a flying leap into what he thought was the side-car. The next moment he got a nasty shock. It wasn't a side-car at all, but a barrow full of eggs for the regiment's breakfast, and the cook chappie didn't think it at all funny. He thought our pal must be an eggs-traordinary fellow to mistake a barrow full of hen fruit for a side-car, and lost no time in telling him so in a loud voice. Then Harold, looking more like an omelette than a soldier, got on his way to the colonel's abode.

4. He hadn't noticed the observation balloon coming along behind him, not having optics in the back of his neck, and he got a bit of a surpruzzle when the hook of same caught in his reach-me-downs and lifted him off terra firma. Harold certainly felt like going up in the air about this latest development, but he didn't feel quite so umpty when the seat of his pants gave way and he was dropped right outside the colonel's abode. When he got inside the prems and handed the piece of paper to the colonel, that worthy gent informed him that it wasn't the password at all, but a pass to the pictures which he was afraid he couldn't use as he was too busy! Pass out of Harold!

79

Vicky the Vacky; Magic; March 1940; (George Drysdale); © D.C. Thomson

EVACUATION SAVES THE NATION!

When the kids left the cities on September the first, 1939, it was a signal for the countryfolk to call the cattle home, lock up the rabbits and hide away the henfruit. The evacuees were on their way, and merry hell was about to break loose. The biggest problem about evacuees was how to spell it, especially, it seems, if you were a comic editor. **Knockout** introduced Our Happy Vaccies, as illustrated by Hugh McNeill, and a week or two later changed them to Our Happy Vakkies. This was finally resolved in the Christmas **Knockout Fun Book**, which called them Our Crazy Kids. **Dandy** did little better with their variant, Vicky the Vacky.

Our Happy Vaccies; Knock-Out; June 1940; (Hugh McNeill); © Amalgamated Press

Our Happy Vaccies; Knock-Out; October 1940; (Hugh McNeill); © Amalgamated Press

OUR HAPPY VAKKIES HIT THE HIGH SPOTS!

Annie Vakkie; Knock-Out; October 1940; (Frank Lazenby); © Amalgamated Press

ANNIE VAKKY WRITES HOME — Read her letter, then turn to page 14 and see if you're right.

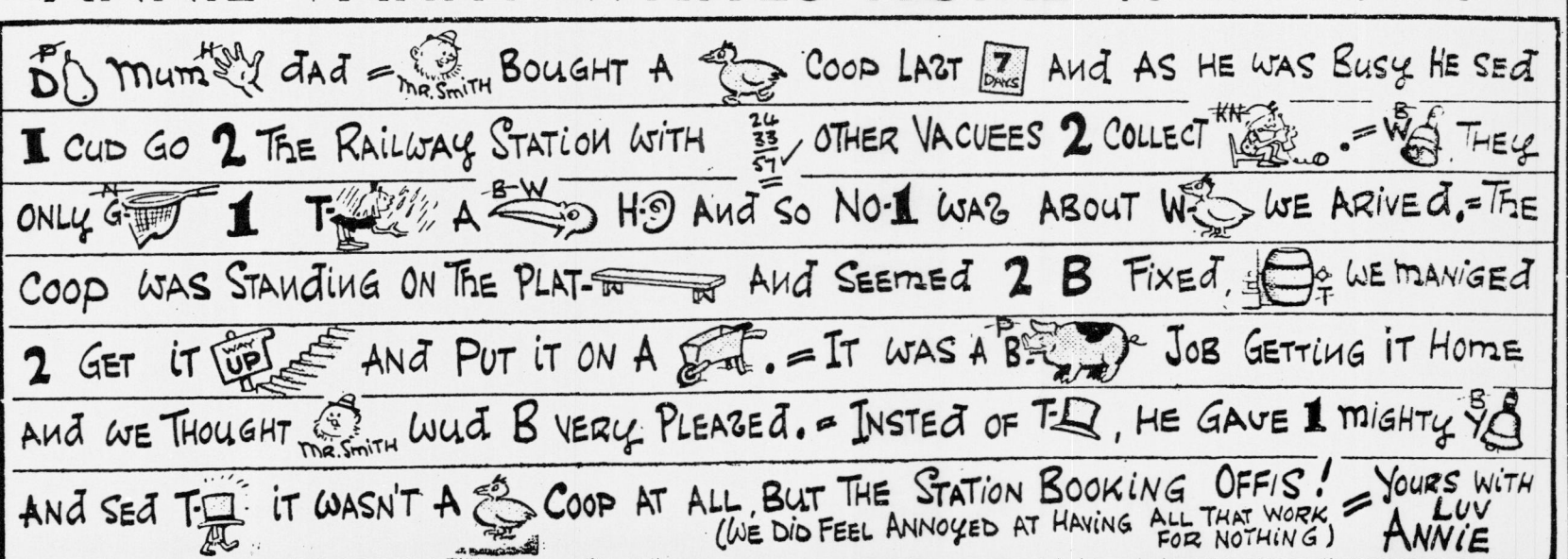

BLACKOUT BLUES!

"Put that light out!" became the first catchphrase of the war, as Air Raid Wardens patrolled the shadowed streets keeping an eye out for chinks in the windows (cue for ancient racist joke!). There had been a few practice blackouts before the declaration, but now they came thick and fast at the rate of one a night. Comics were full of them, too, as cartoonists found them a new source of fun: they were also quick and easy to draw! To help us see our way in the streets at night, the Great White Line was painted down the middle of the nation's roads, giving us a new song hit, 'Follow the White Line', and a new theme for comic strip capers by such young men in uniform as Ben and Bert the Kid Cops.

83

Barney Boko; Dandy; January 1940; (John Mason); © D.C. Thomson

Crusoe Kids; Comic Cuts; July 1940; (Cyril Price); © Amalgamated Press

THE ADVENTURES OF GRANDFATHER CLOCK

"It's black-out time! Get that blind down,"
Says Warden Joe to Tommy Brown.
"We won't," says Tom, "although it's night,
Until you learn to be polite."

Now in the house see that lad come.
He says that he will make things hum.
And just for spite that nasty lout
Gives Tommy's ear a hefty clout

But Grandpa Clock has seen this deed,
And to the lad says, "There's no need
To cut up rough, just 'cos you find
That we forgot to fix the blind."

Joe pulls the blind like anything.
He doesn't know it's on a spring.
And when old Grandpa lets it go
There's trouble for poor Warden Joe.

Young Tommy thinks that it's a treat
To see Joe lifted off his feet.
Joe bawls and shouts, "That is not fair,"
As he's pulled up into the air.

You'll hear Joe more than ever holler
As he goes whizzing round the roller.
And Grandpa starts to smile and beam
As he hits yet another scheme.

He gets his pal, young Lenny Lamp,
To come and help him with this scamp,
"Be quick," says Grandpa, with a frown,
As he and Len lift Joey down.

Now Joe will soon feel very sore.
'Cos Grandpa carts him out the door,
And with a bump he drops that toad,
Who now goes rolling down the road.

Poor Joe ends up against a fence.
He's no more cheek or confidence.
Old Grandpa walks up and says coolly,
"In future, don't be such a bully."

Grandfather Clock; Magic; March 1940; (Alan Fraser); © D.C. Thomson

The Comical Capers of Constable Cuddlecook

1. Dear Mr. Editor, My Gay Old Gherkin,—Willie Whatnot, the Air Raid Warden, walked into the station. "Your lights weren't blacked out properly last night," he said, and Inspector Spadger told me to stick some black paper on our fanlight. "Am I a policeman or a paperhanger?" I said as I climbed on a plank to reach the window. "This makes me feel stuck-up!"

2. Inspector Spadger couldn't find his book of clues. "I wonder where it's got to?" he said, looking up the chimney and behind his ear. Then he spotted it holding my plank up, and with a yell like a Red Indian on the warpath he pulled it from under me. I was left strung up without any visible means of support, and then went sliding down the plank towards Spadger.

3. Spadger got a proper eyeful! Yes, the paste-pot came down from the sky and landed on his head. "Is that a new type of tin helmet?" I asked. Just then the commissioner came along and a gust of wind blew his money away. "Coo! Look what's in the wind!" I said. I grabbed Spadger by his boots and hoisted him into the air. "Grab them" I yelled.

4. All the notes floated through the air and stuck to the inspector, who was feeling properly up in the air about it all. "Bravo, Cuddy!" cried the commissioner, rushing up. We peeled the notes off old Spadger, who looked as if he could do with a wash. "This reminds me of peeling onions, sir!" I laughed. "Seems funny; peeling a peeler!" The commissioner gave me one of the notes. "You can stick to that, Cuddy!" he said.—Yours till crabs wear monocles, CONSTABLE CUDDLECOOK.

GAS MASK DRILL

CAN MAKE YOU ILL!

Gas masks were God's gift to schoolkids in 1939. Not only did gas mask drill fill fifteen minutes that might otherwise have been spent doing sums, wearing the things gave us the only chance we would ever get to blow raspberries at the teacher! This noisome aspect of gas maskery failed to make the funny papers, although the other widespread misuse of the cardboard gas mask case as a portable lunch box proved an obvious wheeze for Hungry Horace. The war penetrated such realms of fantasy as the medieval kingdom ruled by Good King Coke ('He's Stoney Broke'), whose naughty nevvies salted his gas mask with pepper, and the fairyland dwellings of Cinderella and her Ugly Sisters, where the Goblin of the Magic Slipper made gas masks grow legs.

Stan Deezy; Knock-Out; November 1939; (Frank Lazenby); © Amalgamated Press

Hungry Horace; Dandy; December 1941; (Allan Morley); © D.C. Thomson

Deed-A-Day Danny; Knock-Out; October 1944; (A.J. Kelly); © Amalgamated Press

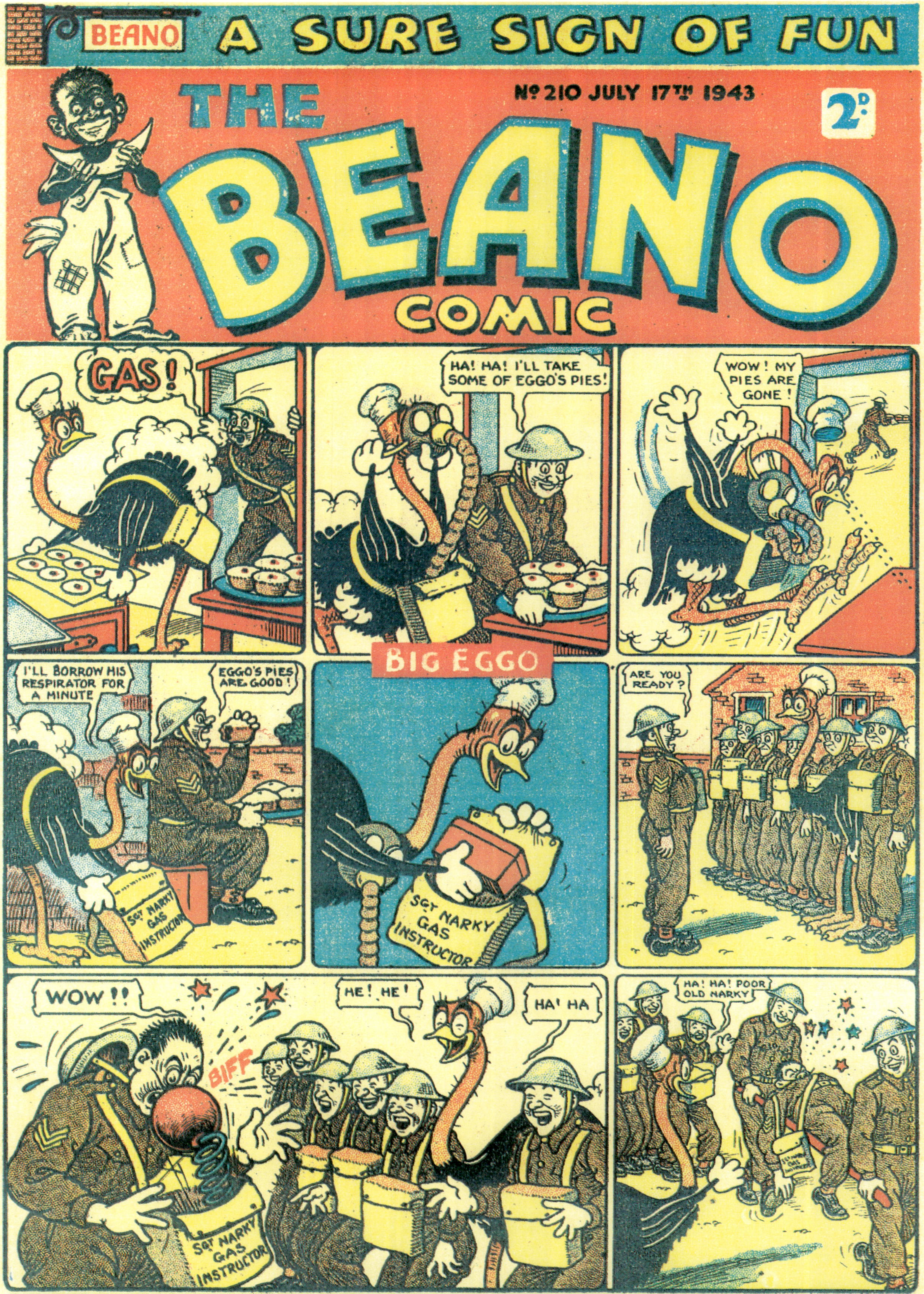

Big Eggo; Beano; July 1943; (Reg Carter); © D.C. Thomson

90

BARRAGE BALLOONS!
– A SKY FULL OF SAUSAGES!

'In Town This Week' was a brilliant series of double-page parodies of the popular BBC radio series, 'In Town Tonight'. Scripted in Billy Bennett-style verses, and comically illustrated by George Parlett, the feature was a favourite in **Radio Fun.** The interviewer, Lionel Grumblin, was based, of course, on Lionel Gamlin. We have already met Militiaman Mulligitawney: now meet Flight Lieutenant Willie Bounce of the Balloon Barrage, a gasbag if ever there was one. City skies were thick with these silvery sausages at the time, so it is small wonder that airborne heroes like Alfie the Air Tramp should collide with them from time to time.

Luke and Len; Larks; December 1939; (Wally Robertson); © Amalgamated Press

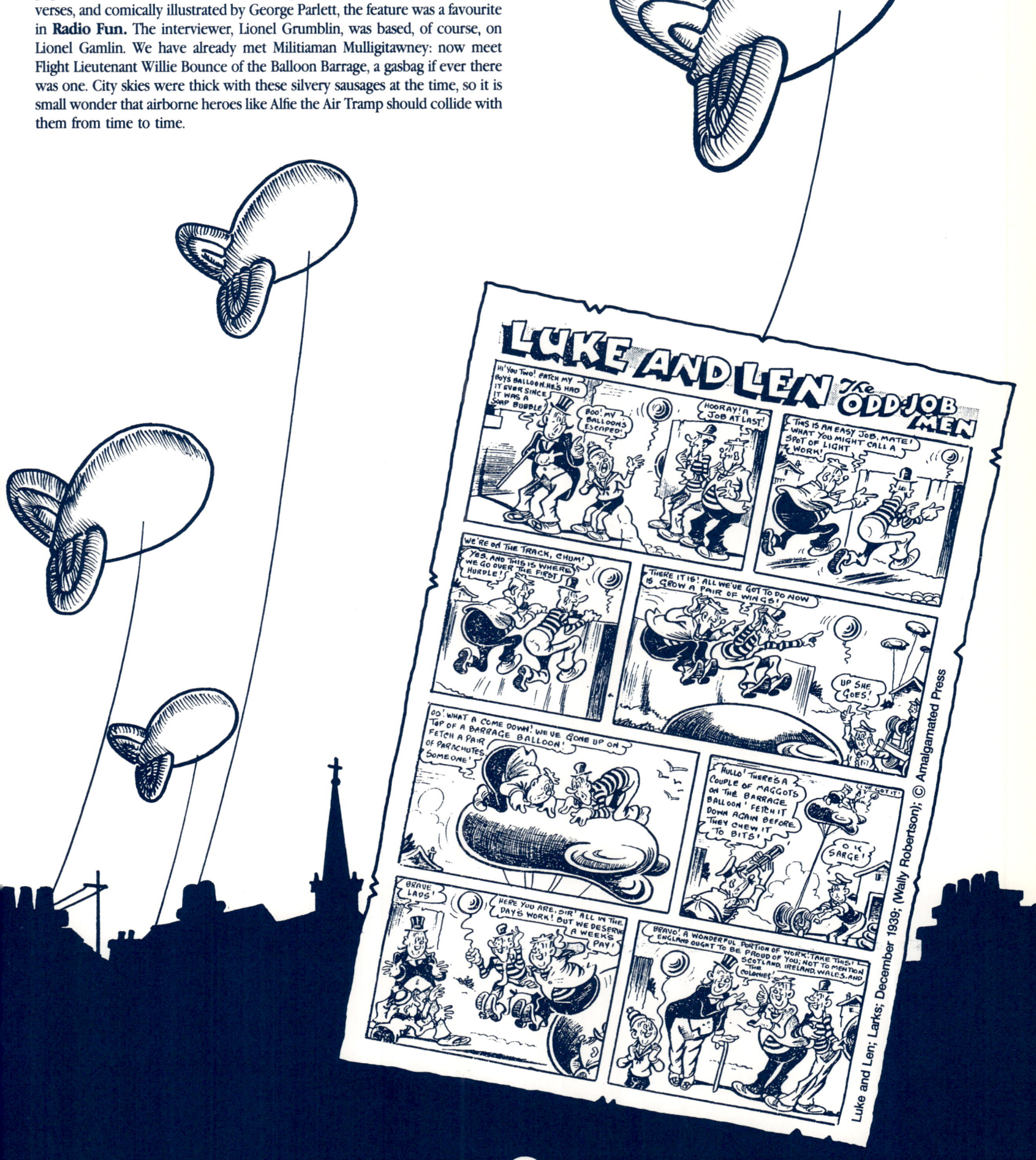

IT'S THE GREMLINS!

1. The Gremlins wanted more eggs, so they bought some chicks and started an egg-factory. 'Twas grand fun, chums, until Harry Hawk tried to add to his meat ration with a spot of poultry. Again and again, our Gremlins beat him to it and beat him off. It got a bit too much for them, so they called a Cabinet meeting near the hen-house. "Dive bombing! That's what it is!" cried Bignut. "We need a barrage balloon!" Well, of course, it was no sooner said than done. Our Gremlins are like that! Besides, they saw fun in it.

2. And such a nifty balloon they made, too! 'Twas proper patchwork and crazy paving. Everybody was happy, except Willy Winder in the cage with the cable. Funnyboy tempted him with a sausage and made rude remarks. Clara Cluck got on top of it, somehow, and tried to look as if she'd laid it, but nobody believed her. It was a good idea to be prepared for Harry Hawk's next visit, but a stitch in time is a stitch too much when it's in your pants. Both Rookie and Sam Simp got caught up that way. Maybe the thing will go pop, but who cares. They'll have fun again next week.

Alfie the Air Tramp; Chips; May 1941; (John Jukes); © Amalgamated Press

IN TOWN THIS WEEK!

Good-evening, everybody! This is RADIO FUN'S private studio broadcasting to the world and also America! To-day Lionel Grumblin interviews yet another of the interesting personalities who are "IN TOWN THIS WEEK." Here we have Willie Bounce of the Balloon Barrage to tell you all about his job. Funny thing is you have to have the "wind-up" to be any good at it at all! Shush, here they are!

"Good evening — how do, everybody? Lionel Grumblin of Radio Renown, will chat to a chap from the Air Force — Willie Bounce (Flight Lieutenant) is in town!

Now Willie's a bit of a gasbag it's in Balloon Barrage he serves — he sends airships and things up in sky on long strings — he likes them — like him they're all curves!

Mr. Bounce has just finished refreshment — he's put down his saucer and cup, he looks like a balloon and he'll speak to us soon, so stand by 'cos the balloon's just gone up!

"How d'you do, listeners-in, I'm an airman, I'm a flier who stays safe and sound, in the sky I don't fly 'cos the sky's much too high so I keep trotters well on the ground!

Your pop and your mum, if you ask 'em, will remember the Fat Boy of Peckham — a stout fella he, but a rake beside me, when I get in folks' cars, why I wreck 'em!

LAST GASP!

As a baby I flattened my go-cart, I don't mean perhaps or just maybe —

— and one day in my cot my mum said "Willie's not! That boy is a fine bouncing baby!"

CRUNCH! BOUNCE!

At three I was blowing big bubbles, I watched them as upwards they flew right into the sky and a cute lad was I, 'cos I brightly said "Da! and Goo Goo!"

My favourite toy was a big airball, I'd a squeaker and fat 'dying pig', but my games with such toys were soon stopped by big boys, armed with pins, — they were all 'infra dig'!

POP!

When I was a little bit older, my Pa, (that is him, wearing bowler) said "A big boy like that can help me get lawn flat, so I spent my spare time as a roller!

After my twenty-first birthday — I was pumping up Dad's car one day, — Balloon tyres it had and I shouted out "Dad! What a lovely big b'loon, ain't it, eh?"

Then the old country called for assistance, for balloons I felt I'd quite a gift, so I went to enlist and the Flight-Sergeant hissed, "Good gracious — balloon's broke adrift!"

They entered me as an Aircraftman the open-air life made me tough, — Balloons I inflated, 'twas a job that I hated — When I'd finished I'd lost all my puff!

I asked them to give me promotion — Squadron-Leader he said no at first — cried he "Now dismiss!" But I said "You mark this — I'll blow up your balloons till they burst!"

An officer they quickly made me — They gave me a sword and a nag — My job, so they say, if a balloon runs away is to chase it and prod the gasbag!

Lionel's asked me the use of this barrage, why we send up balloons in a fleet — Well, in a very few words it's to give dicky birds a nice place to rest their poor feet!

Inspections we've held by the dozen — Of reviews we have several scores my balloons, all in line, with chests out look just fine, — I'm the one shouting "Gasbags, form fours!"

"Well, this has been most interesting, — Mr. Airman, you must now dine with me — Let me buy you some pop and some air-pie, old top, you will get a good blow-out all free!"

NEXT WEEK: — Lionel Grumblin will interview Freddie the Footballer.

'TUNING UP THE A.R.P.!

The initials A.R.P. stood for Air Raid Precautions, but A.R.P. Wardens stood for no nonsense – except in the comics! For comic artists found a whole new world of wonderful fun in the paraphernalia of A.R.P. wardenry: buckets of water, buckets of sand, sandbags, air raid shelters, tin hats, whistles, stirrup-pumps, all were grist to the cartoonist's mill. For a catalogue of comicality, peruse the pages George Parlett devoted to Wally the Warden in his hilarious spoof, 'In Town This Week'. A.R.P. was all about air raids, of course, and once these started in earnest even bombs became high explosive hilarity for the likes of Our Ernie, Lord Snooty and his Pals and, quite surprisingly, the Tickler Twins in Wonderland.

Deed-A-Day Danny; Knock-Out; October 1941; (Hugh McNeill); © Amalgamated Press

Big Eggo; Beano; August 1943; (Reg Carter); © D.C. Thomson

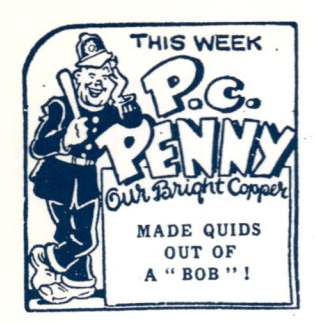

P.C. Penny; Comic Cuts; November 1939; (Cyril Price); © Amalgamated Press

BEN AND BERT BAG SOME BAGS AND MAKE A GENT FOOT THE BILL.

Ben and Bert; Funny Wonder; October 1939; (Harry Parlett); © Amalgamated Press

MARMY AND MA HAVE A DUST-UP OVER SOME RUBBISH.

Marmy and his Ma; Funny Wonder; November 1939; (Wally Robertson); © Amalgamated Press

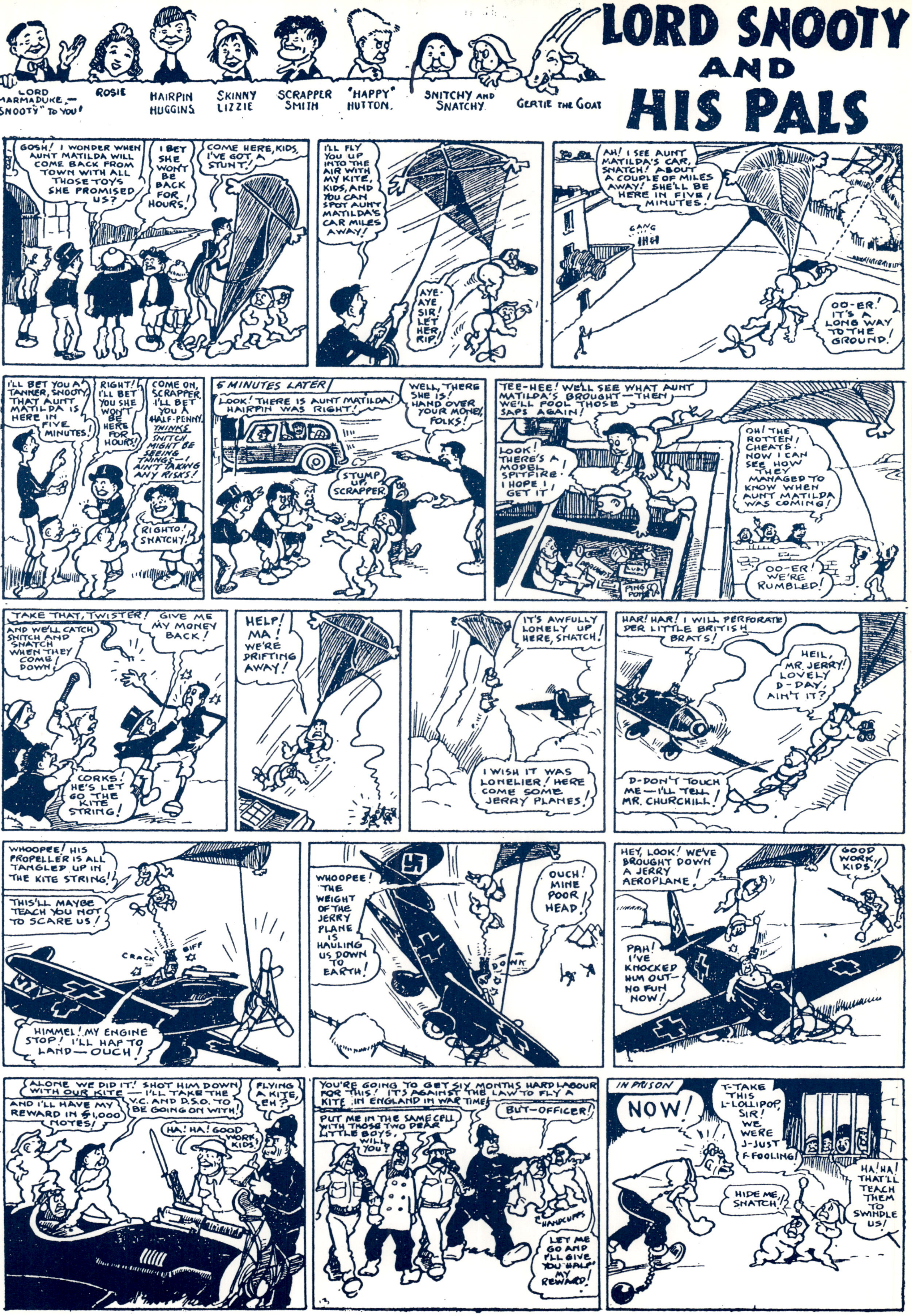

Lord Snooty; Beano; July 1943; (Dudley Watkins); © D.C. Thomson

A Nazi spoils the Twins' plum duff, but soon that Nazi's brooding—

THE TICKLER TWINS

In a paper, the Ticklers see
Some news that fills them full of glee.
Some lads are offering a prize
For a plum duff of enormous size.

Says Mick to Trix, "Our fortune's made.
We'll put the others in the shade."
And soon those kids are out of puff
As they stir up that huge plum duff.

They get a huge bowl on the ground
And pop in raisins by the pound,
They also put in loads of flour.
Mick says, "We'll finish it in an hour."

But Trixie nearly has a fit
When she is pouring into it
Some baking soda, with great care—
She hears a noise up in the air.

An aeroplane she now sees coming.
Towards them at full speed it's humming.
It's a German by the looks of things,
For it's got crosses on its wings.

Young Trixie Tickler gets a fright.
She drops the soda which lands right
Inside the duff—so just look out!
What happens will make Micky shout.

They put that duff now with a grin
In a mighty oven made of tin,
And then the Twins turn on the heat
But soon with fear they start to bleat.

Because when baking soda's hot
It makes things rise up on the spot,
So now the duff and oven rise
Although they're of such mighty size.

The Tickler Twins hang on like glue
And they go floating skywards too.
But soon they bring it down once more,
And pop it in the oven door.

The Tickler Twins; Magic; December 1940; (Bob MacGillivray; © D.C. Thomson

100

'Cos he's shot down when they go flying on their Christmas pudding!

But soon Mick has a dandy scheme
That makes his little sister beam.
"Open the oven," hear Mick shout,
"I'll catch that duff when it floats out."

When that duff comes he will lasso it—
He's got some rope that ought to do it.
Out it comes now, piping hot
And Micky lassoes it first shot.

With some more rope he does his stuff.
Now you won't recognise that duff
'Cos soon it's like a flying boat.
So up in it the Ticklers float.

As up into the air they soar
That Nazi now appears once more.
He sees the plum duff and he says,
"Oh dear! I ain't had grub for days."

He tries to pinch some with a spoon
But soon the Twins make that lad swoon.
'Cos Micky throws a rolling pin
And knocks his 'plane quite outside in.

He bales out in his parachute—
For him the Twins were far too cute.
They now tuck in and have a feed
And have a merry time indeed.

OUR ERNIE

MRS. ENTWHISTLE'S LITTLE LAD.

As Ernie sat in bed one night
(The room were lit by candle light)
He made a hefty dog appear
On bed-room wall. It did look queer!

Then looking out into the night,
He saw a searchlight, clear and bright.
Cried lad: "By gum, I think I'll try
My luck with shadowgraph on sky!"

So off he toddled through the night,
And came at last to searchlight site;
And no one shouted "Halt!" or "Stop!"
'Cos sentry had gone for glass of pop.

So Ernie put his hands together,
And on a bit of cloudy weather
Appeared a bomber, flying high,
A Nasti one—using our sky!

Cried colonel of gun battery,
"Wow! Where's my specs? What's this I see?
A Nasti using our nice night?
Make guns go bang, men! Give him fright!"

And you can bet the gunners did,
Not knowing 'twere the work of kid
Nor that where cloud the night-sky hid,
A bunch of Nasti gliders glid.

'Twere Tickler's great invasion plan.
And on those gliders every man
Were armed to teef, and filled wiv glee
To think at last they'd crossed our sea.

But just when they were shouting "Heil!"
And holding hands up—Nasti style,
Bang! Crash! 'Twere nasty shock for Fritz—
His glider planes just fell to bits.

Meanwhile a sergeant came to tell
The searchlight men that they'd been swell,
But finding Ernie, got quite wild
And said some norty words to child.

But at that moment, from the cloud,
It started raining Nasti crowd,
And colonel cried: "Why, Ernie, fanks
To you, we've captured men and tanks!

"You're hero, lad. Please take reward—
Take what you like—except my sword—
Take tin hat, tank, or motor-bike—
Or German sausage—what you like!"

Cried Ernie: "Eh, I think I'll bone
A prisoner, for my very own,
And also tank, so I can run,
A private war and have some fun!"

Our Ernie; Knock-Out; August 1941; (Hugh McNeill); © Amalgamated Press

102

Lord Snooty; Beano; September 1943; (Dudley Watkins); © D.C. Thomson

Tootsy McTurk; Magic; October 1940; (John Mason); © D.C. Thomson

Deed-A-Day Danny; Knock-Out; June 1942; (Wally Robertson); © Amalgamated Press

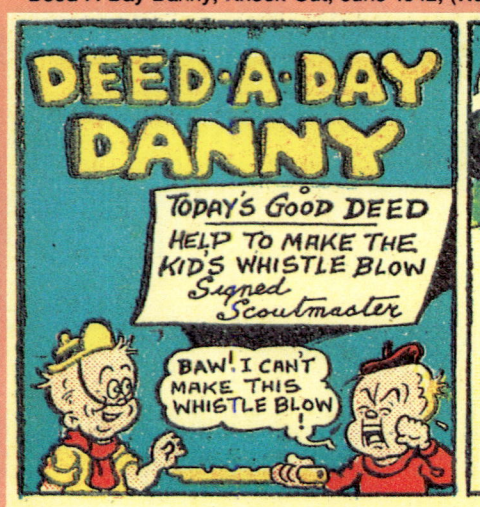

104

BOY BIFFO THE BRAVE

ONE BIFF SLEW NINE

Into a town Boy Biffo's strayed
And landed slap in an air-raid.
So while the bombers circle o'er
Biffo's shoved in a shelter's door!

Air-raids are new ones on Biffo,
'Cos there were no planes long ago.
But here are airmen, and they fly,
On giant crows all o'er the sky!

With rotten eggs they bomb the town,
And the warden mutters with a frown,
"They're Wizard Wittler's men, and they
Bomb this town near every day."

To find out more see Biffo spy
Upon the Wizard's house nearby.
His monster pets the Wizard feeds
With—here's the secret!—magic seeds.

The crows tuck in and in a tick
They start to grow up mighty quick!
But while old Wittler's turned his back
Boy Biffo grabs the birds' seed sack!

"There won't be any more giant crows!"
Biffo thinks as to town he goes.
But that sack bursts as home he speeds—
And sparrows eat the magic seeds!

Right into town Boy Biffo's followed
By monster sparrows who have swallowed
The magic seeds. The townsfolk crow,
"We'll lick Wiz Wittler now, Biffo!"

And so, when next the bombers come
There's fighters there to make things hum.
And mounted on a chirpy sparrow
Biffo flies at them like an arrow.

They drop bricks on each pilot's crown
And soon the bombers are all down.
Gosh! The folks cheer till they're hoarse
For Biffo and his new Air Force!

Boy Biffo the Brave; Magic; November 1940; (Sam Fair); © D.C. Thomson

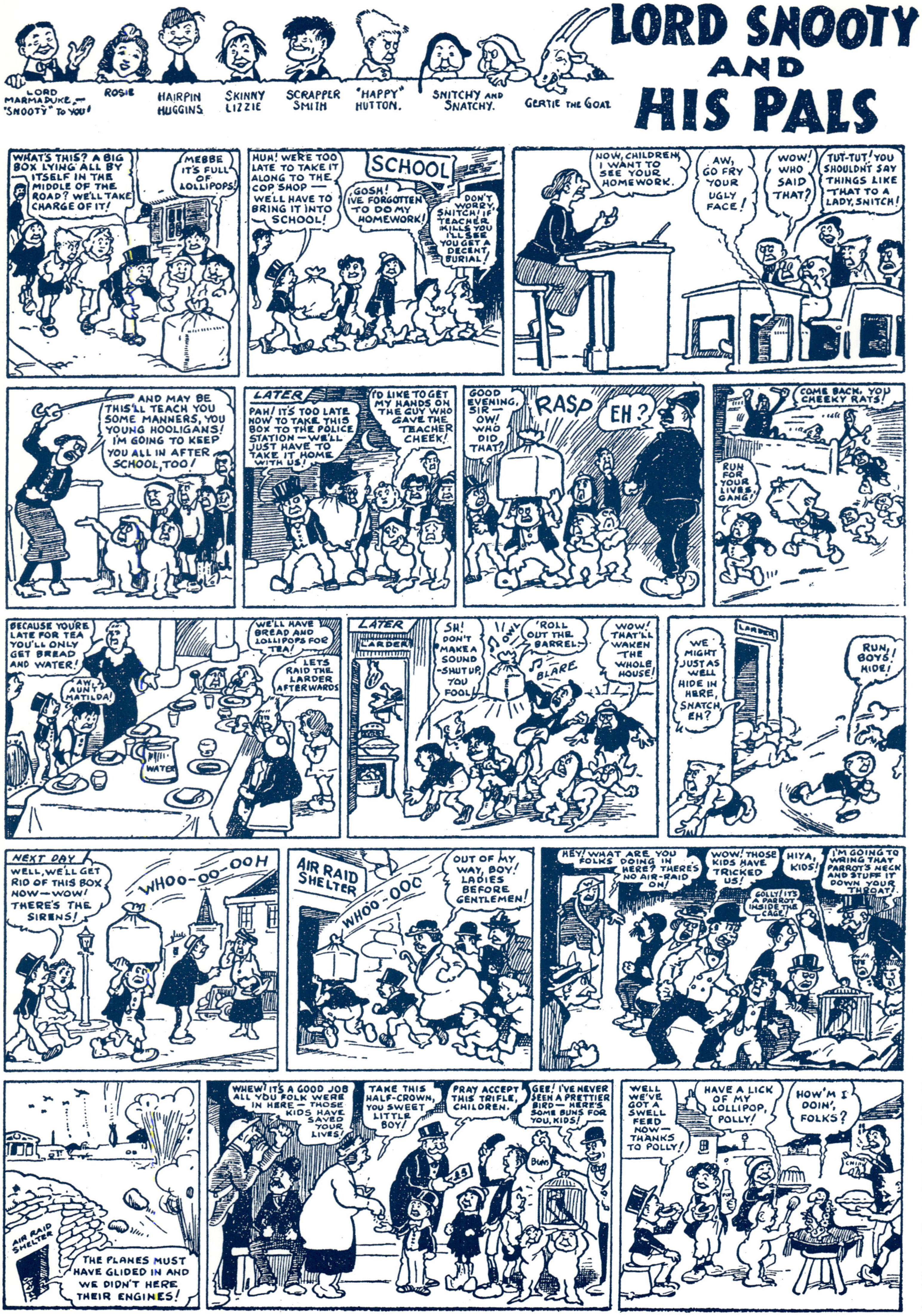

Lord Snooty; Beano; November 1943; (Dudley Watkins); © D.C. Thomson

PA PERKINS AND HIS SON PERCY

1. "What-ho! I must be the cleverest A. R. Peanut around here," purred Pa Perkins to little Percy, as he showed off his latest gadget. "See the idea, sonny boy? Non-stop from bed-room to garden shelter!"

2. "Marvellous, Pa!" crooned Percy. "You certainly have got brains." "Oh, I've got some that I haven't even used yet!" guffed Pa, with modest pride. "I'll go and get the warden to see this work of wonder."

3. But when Pa toddled off, little Percy decided that there was money in the bright brainwave. "Here you are, kids!" he carolled. "This way for the slippery slide!" And the kids galloped up in gladsome style.

4. Having brought the warden along to the scene of the great invention, Pa proceeded to say his little piece. "You see, sir," he tootled. "Scoot down the chute and you don't care a hoot! Brilliant, isn't it?"

5. Then—swish! Down came the kids for slippery cruise, and poor old Pa stopped a pair of boots with his pants. "Gosh! Attack from the rear!" he gasped.

6. "Take cover, warden!" Then head-first into the shelter went Pa, while the lads continued their slide, and the air warden went home. He'd seen enough!

Deed-A-Day Danny; Knock-Out; November 1939; (Hugh McNeill); © Amalgamated Press

Deed-A-Day Danny; Knock-Out; September 1942; (Norman Ward); © Amalgamated Press

IN TOWN THIS WEEK!

Hallo, everybody. Once more Lionel Grumblin stops the mighty roar of London's traffic. Only this time there isn't such a mighty roar to stop because there's a black-out on! But Lionel brings to the microphone WALLY THE AIR-RAID WARDEN who will tell you the great adventures he has in his A.R.P. work. There goes the red light! Shush. Lionel has just coughed. That means he is going to start his interview.

LIONEL GRUMBLIN IS HERE ONCE AGAIN, FOLK, I'M GOING TO BURST INTO RHYME,— THIS BROADCAST WILL START IN A MINUTE, BUT FIRST LET LARGE BENJAMIN CHIME!

IN THESE DAYS OF CONFUSION AND TROUBLE THE A.R.P. PEOPLE ARE MUSTERED AND WALLY THE WARDEN IS WITH US — HE'S JUST KNOCKING BACK A QUICK CUSTARD!

"HOW-DE-DO, PALS, I'M WALLY THE WARDEN, FOLK FEEL SAFE WHEN THEY HEAR ME AROUND —

— IF A BOMB DROPS NEAR ME I JUST PICK IT UP, SEE? SAYING 'LUVVUS! JUST LOOK WHAT I'VE FOUND!"

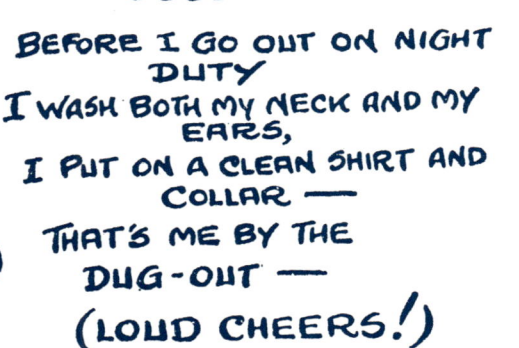

I USED TO BE QUITE GOOD AT JUGGLING, SO IF IN THE STREET YOU SHOULD SEE A CHAP WHO, FOR FUN, TOSSES BOMBS (P'RAPS DROPS ONE), TIS A SAFE BET THAT CHAPPIE IS ME!

BEFORE I GO OUT ON NIGHT DUTY I WASH BOTH MY NECK AND MY EARS, I PUT ON A CLEAN SHIRT AND COLLAR — THAT'S ME BY THE DUG-OUT — (LOUD CHEERS!)

I'M FUSSY ABOUT MY APPEARANCE — IN THE CITY I DRESS LIKE A SWELL —

— MY AIR-WARDEN'S REGALIA WAS MADE BY MY 'TAILIAH' IT FITS, WHERE IT TOUCHES, QUITE WELL!

In Town This Week; Radio Fun; October 1939; (George Parlett); © Amalgamated Press

BEFORE A·R·P WAS INVENTED, I LEARNED ABOUT GAS IN THIS WAY – A LEAK I HAD SOUGHT WITH A CANDLE I'D BOUGHT –
CELLAR
GAS
SS-SS
– AND THEY PICKED ME UP TWO MILES AWAY!
BOOM
MY TIN HAT IS EVER SO HANDY APART FROM IT'S USE ON MY HEAD. AS A DISH IT'S A GOOD 'UN WHEN FULL OF RICE PUDDEN, OR FOR FAG-ENDS WHEN I SMOKE IN BED!
A.R.P
I SAW AN OLD GIRL IN AN AIR RAID, (PLEASE DON'T THINK THAT I'D EVER BELITTLE HER), SHE SAID "MR. WALLY – JUST LOOK AT MY BROLLY! I SHALL WRITE A STIFF NOTE TO YOUNG HITLER!"
BIFF!
DUGOUT
ARP
NORSES.
WHEN AN ENEMY AIRPLANE COMES OVER, AN AERIAL TORPEDO HE DROPS, BUT I CATCH SAME IN CAP –
PLONK
ARP
AND BUZZ IT BACK IN HIS LAP –
ARP
AND A LARGE LUMP OF TROUBLE HE COPS!
ACH!
WELL, THANK YOU FOR ALL YOU HAVE TOLD US, YOU'VE MADE US FEEL ALL BRAVE AND CALM – WILL YOU SHOW US HOW BEST TO TAKE COVER ON HEARING THE AIR RAID ALARM?
PARP
PARP
STEEL SAFE (TOUGH AS OLD BOOTS)
A·R·P
NOW THAT WAS MOST PROMPT AND EFFECTIVE – I'VE SOUNDED THE ALL CLEAR ONCE MORE, BUT I REGRET TO CONFIDE THAT THE KEY IS INSIDE AND YOU'VE JUST SLAMMED A SELF-LOCKING DOOR!"
STEEL SAFE TOUGH AS OLD BOOTS

WOW! WOMEN OF WAR!

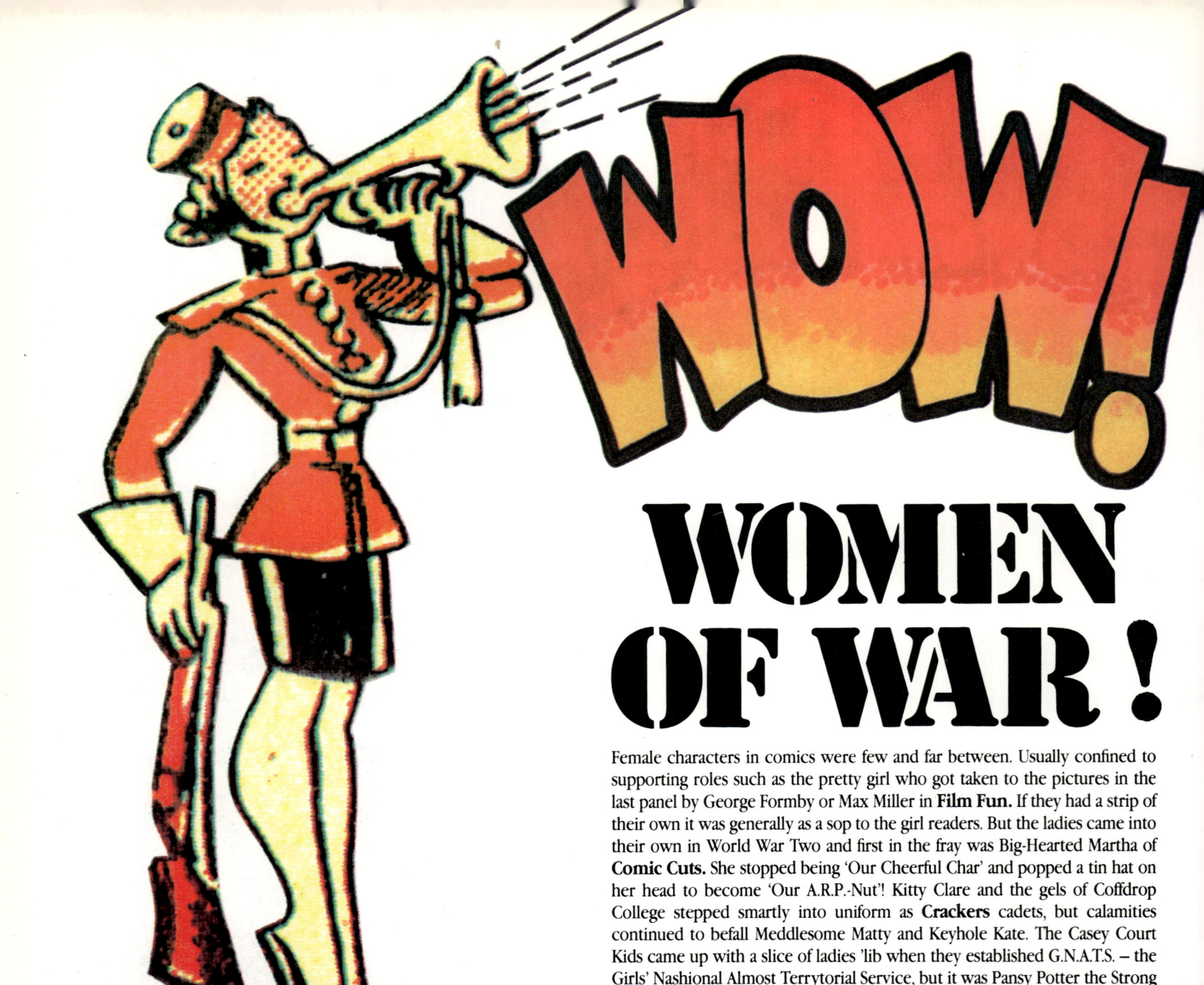

Female characters in comics were few and far between. Usually confined to supporting roles such as the pretty girl who got taken to the pictures in the last panel by George Formby or Max Miller in **Film Fun.** If they had a strip of their own it was generally as a sop to the girl readers. But the ladies came into their own in World War Two and first in the fray was Big-Hearted Martha of **Comic Cuts.** She stopped being 'Our Cheerful Char' and popped a tin hat on her head to become 'Our A.R.P.-Nut'! Kitty Clare and the gels of Coffdrop College stepped smartly into uniform as **Crackers** cadets, but calamities continued to befall Meddlesome Matty and Keyhole Kate. The Casey Court Kids came up with a slice of ladies 'lib when they established G.N.A.T.S. – the Girls' Nashional Almost Terrytorial Service, but it was Pansy Potter the Strong Man's Daughter who really liberated girl readers of **The Beano** with her all-out action against Jerry submarines.

Keyhole Kate; Dandy; August 1941; (Allan Morley); © D.C. Thomson.

Meddlesome Matty; Dandy; May 1942; (Sam Fair); © D.C. Thomson.

Dolly Dimple; Magic; September 1940; (Allan Morley); © D.C. Thomson.

Tell Tale Tilly; Magic; July 1940; (George Drysdale); © D.C. Thomson.

Casey Court; Chips; December 1939; (Albert Pease); © Amalgamated Press.

This week the lads of Casey Court have taken a back seat, because the girls have come to the front with big ideas of doing their bit these days. All the lasses joined the G.N.A.T.S., and they certainly made things buzz in the neighbourhood. "This is a gnatty notion, girls," said Sally Trotters, who started the whole business. "Who'll volunteer to be a patient for the bandaging practice?" Micky Smiff said he didn't mind a job like that—but he was certainly wrapped up in his work!

Peggy the Pride of the Force; Larks; December 1939; (George Parlett); © Amalgamated Press.

Pansy Potter; Beano; August 1940; (Basil Blackaller); © D.C. Thomson.

Big Hearted Martha; Comic Cuts; April 1940; (Cyril Price); © Amalgamated Press.

115

Kitty Clare; Crackers; May 1940; (Bertie Brown); © Amalgamated Press.

KITTY CLARE'S SCHOOLDAYS.

"Oh, what an honour for Coffdrop College!" cooed Miss Allchin, as the voice at the other end of the telephone told her that a general was coming along for her inspection. "We must get ready for the inspection at once!" she said to the girls. And as Kitty Clare and Podgy and Skittles ran out to fall in, Miss Allchin went to her room and put on the uniform of a Commander-in-Chief of the Fire Guards.

Then Kitty blew "The First Post" on her bugle, and Miss Allchin came stepping out. But it was rather unlucky for her when, instead of stepping on her feet, she stepped on her dangling sword and tripped over it. Splosh! she landed in a puddle. "Is that the way you want us to fall in, Teacher?" piped Podgy. "If so, I think we'd better put on our bathing-suits, don't you?" "Look, here's a lady to see you!" Kitty called just then. Miss Allchin looked round, and who do you think was there—the general SERVANT! What a mistake to make!

Kitty Clare; Crackers; October 1940; (Bertie Brown); © Amalgamated Press.

KITTY CLARE'S SCHOOLDAYS.

There may have been fairies at the bottom of the garden at Coffdrop College, but there was certainly a nice store of food which Fat Podgy had put there. "I don't care about ration books now!" she cooed. "I can come and help myself from my hoard when I feel like it!" And she was so pleased with herself that she went to help Kitty Clare and Skittles clear up the Autumn leaves. "Now I'll play a joke on Kitty!" she smirked.

"How'd you like to go for a nice trip, Kitty?" she giggled. And Kitty did go for a trip—right across the broom. This made her upset all the leaves in her sack, but Miss Allchin didn't mind. "Leave the leaves where they are!" she said. "I'll just set light to them!" But when she did, there was a loud yell from Podgy. "Why, what's the matter?" cried Miss Allchin. Well, it was just a little matter of Podgy's burnt-up cake!

Pansy Potter; Beano; July 1943; (Basil Blackaller); © D.C. Thomson.

Meddlesome Matty; Dandy; January 1940; (Sam Fair); © D.C. Thomson.

DOING THEIR BEST!
ON GUARD WITH THE HOME GUARD!

Originally called the L.D.V. – the Local Defence Volunteers for long – by the time this very British band of blokes marched into the comics they had been better branded the Home Guard. First to hear the call was Tootsy McTurk of **The Magic Comic**, a funny freak for whom the song, 'The Flat Foot Floogie with the Floy Floy', might well have been composed. The Casey Court nibs were not far behind, cantering across the back page of **Chips** in the charge of Billy Baggs, who qualified as Hossifer-in-Chief because he was the only one who owned a monocle! Another odd recruit, with the accent on the odd, was Big Eggo, **Beano's** page one ostrich who soon ousted Austerreich. Lord Snooty's Pals' encounter with the Home Guard was unique, featuring as it did a salute to Stalingrad.

Tootsy McTurk; Magic; November 1940; (John Mason); © D.C. Thomson.

Casey Court; Chips; September 1940; (Albert Pease); © Amalgamated Press.

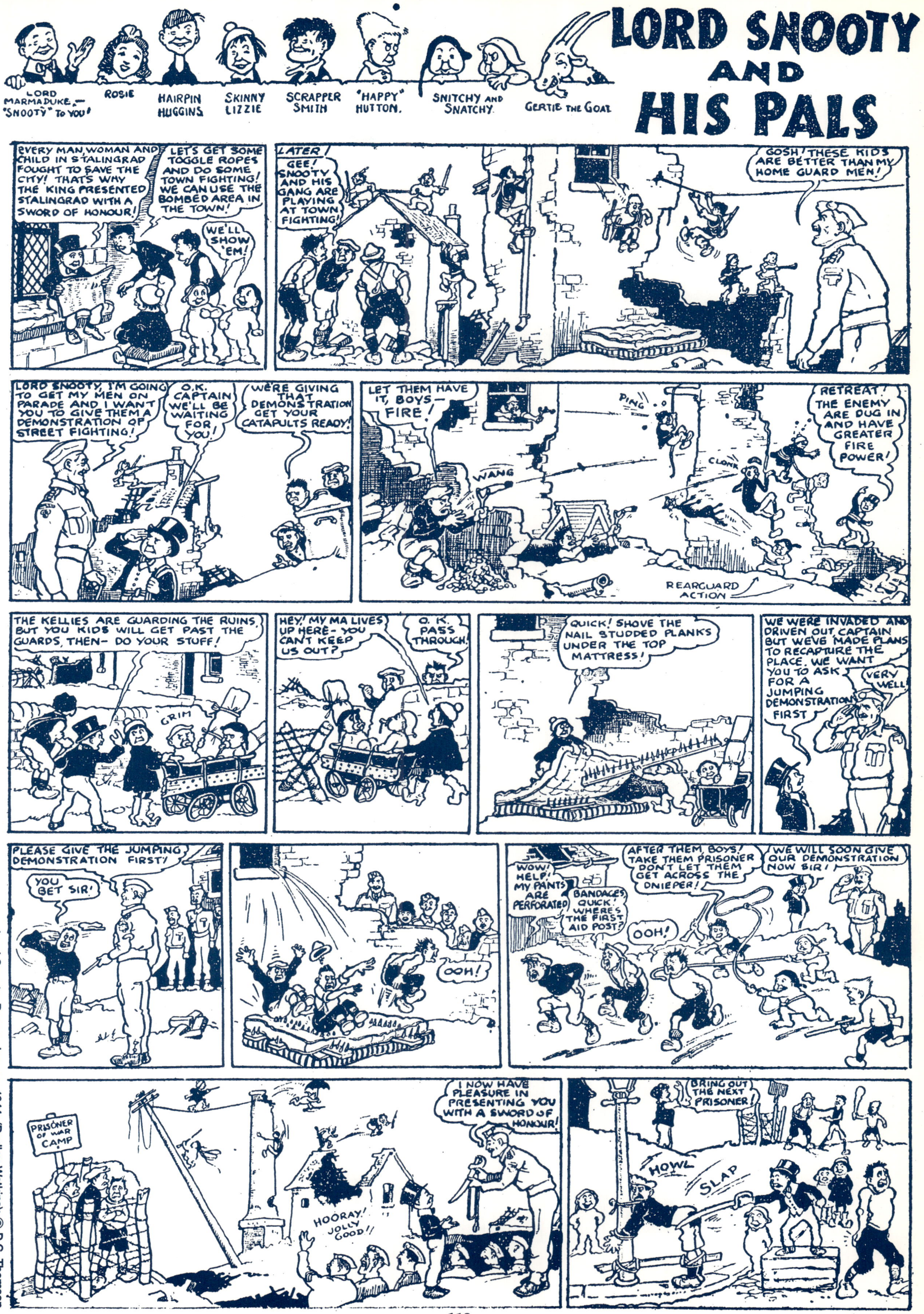

Lord Snooty; Beano; January 1944; (Dudley Watkins); © D.C. Thomson.

Deed-A-Day Danny; Knock-Out; May 1944; (A.J. Kelly); © Amalgamated Press.

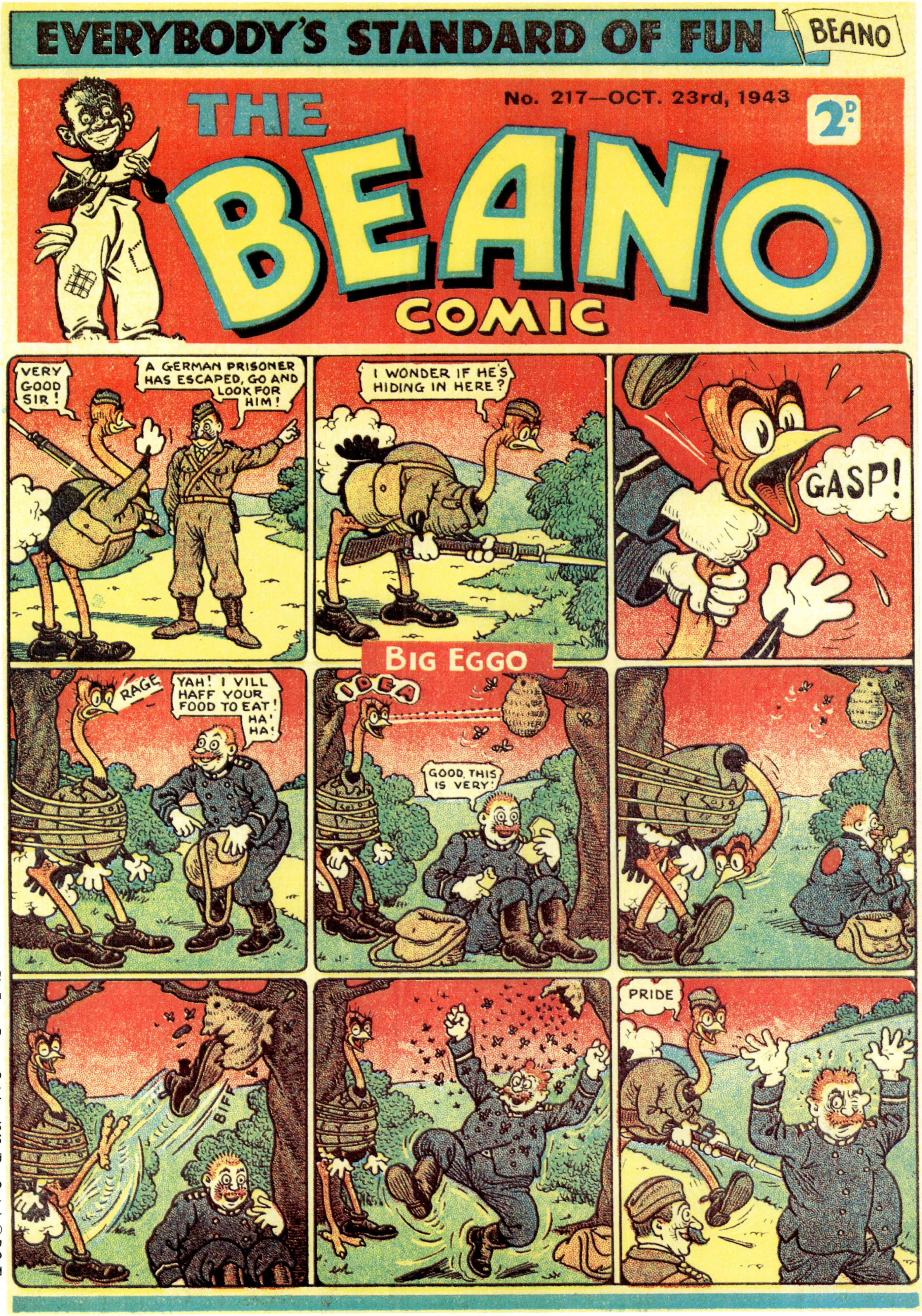

Big Eggo: Beano: October 1943; (Reg Carter); © D.C. Thomson.

HOP IT, HITLER!

INVADERS AND PARACHUTISTS!
★ ★ ★

Invasion was in the air in 1940 – and so were parachutists! Rumour had it that the Nazis were dropping from the skies in the guise of nuns. Keep your eyes on the skies, we were told – and we did – mainly to see what nuns had up their skirts! The invasion threat was a deadly serious one, but not in the comics. After all, if Stonehenge Kit the Ancient Brit and Glam his Gal Pal had repelled General Wusso and his Ancient Romans some several centuries ago, then we could certainly do ditto. Another symbolic invasion took place on the tropical isle of Bamboo Town, where Bongo and Pongo the educated apes soon enlisted the animals to oust a black-faced Hitler. Invasion exercises on British beaches were also good for a laugh, especially if like Pansy Potter you made the obvious mistake.

Bamboo Town; Dandy; September 1940; (Chick Gordon); © D.C. Thomson.

Sandy and Muddy; Knock-Out; December 1940; (Bill Radford); © Amalgamated Press.

Pansy Potter; Beano; May 1941; (Basil Blackaller); © D.C. Thomson.

Sooty Snowball; Magic; October 1940; (Bob MacGillivray); © D.C. Thomson.

Hair Oil Al; Dandy; November 1940 (Artist Unknown); © D.C. Thomson.

STONEHENGE KIT - THE ANCIENT BRIT.

1. King Kongo called a royal conference. A p.c. from his prime-minister said that the Ancient Romans were coming to invade Stonehenge. Kingy hadn't sent them an invite, so what was to be done?

2. It was a to-do, and no three ways about it. Kit told Kingy not to worry his royal nut. They had to go to it! They'd make lots of ammunish and stop the Romans roamin' in the gloamin'.

3. Kingy made Kit a Knight of the Day-Shift at the royal munition factory. Kit commenced work pronto, and was soon shovelling out the shells. Then three tough guys arrived at the factory.

4. They offered to job any job that was going. Kit told them to wipe their feet on the mat and start work. But instead of wiping, they swiped. They were Whizzy and his Brit-bashers.

5. Ding! Dong! Down came cudgels on the crusts of Kit and King Kongo. Whizzy had come to find out the secrets and sell them to the enemy. Now the coast was clear!

6. Kingy curled up on the floor. Kit fell on a moving belt that carried him towards the Ammunish Mixer-Upper. Whizzy chortled at that. It saved him a lot of trouble.

7. A moving scene then followed. Kit was carried into the mixer, while Kingy was carted off by the Brit-bashers. Just outside, Whizzy spotted a shell popping forth.

8. This shell was a Stonehenge Special. Whizzy told his men to bring it along to the beach. The wicked wizard was sure that the Romans would pay him well for the shell.

9. Whizzy chortled as he did a dekko at his pocket sundial. The invasion was now due! Off he cantered to the coast with his Brit-bashers carrying Kingy and the special shell.

10. The Ancient Romans had arrived! Whizzy showed them his captures and ordered Nit and Wit to take the top from the shell. General Wusso was expecting a big surprise.

11. He got one! So did Whizzy and his left-hand men! Out of the shell shot Kit, and he handed headaches all round with a spanner and a wrench. General Wusso was wild at this.

12. The Roman conked Whizzy with a cudgel and called the invasion off. Kit and Kingy chortled. Being shoved inside that shell had saved the day, but there's more fun, next week!

Stonehenge Kit; Knock-Out; January 1942; (Bill Radford); © Amalgamated Press.

125

I SPY MIT MEIN LITTLE EYE!

Spies ran rampant on the comic pages: they made a useful change from bad hats and footpads for the likes of Laurie and Trailer, Chip's comic pair of Secret Service Men who swapped trilby and bowler for caps peaked and forage and joined the proper army – if you call the Coldcream Guards proper! Something even odder occurred to their lifelong enemies Crown Prince Oddsockz and Serge Pantz. These Russkis suddenly switched nationalities and language to become nasty Nazis! Fifth Columnists soon became the buzz-word for foreign agents, but this didn't stop one jolly Jerry from starring in a strip of his own: Herr Paul Pry the Nasty Spy.

LAURIE AND TRAILER — THE SECRET SERVICE MEN

1. Maud and Maisie, the major's daughters waved toodle-oo to Laurie and Trailer, who were toddling into the canteen for a gargle o' grapefruit. "Nice girls, guv'nor," chirped Trailer. Meanwhile, Oddy and Serge were plotting.

2. Our Secret Service lads felt sad when they saw a sad-looking old soul outside, singing for coppers. "Poor chap, he looks hungry," cried Laurie.

3. "I will tempt a smile back to his face with a penny bun." "Har! And I vill put a bump on his topknot wiz my bonker," cackled Serge.

4. But as Serge handed out a free headache Laurie pulled the singer sideways, and 'twas he who stopped the biff!

5. This made him feel very much off song, and it caused his whiskers to do a sideslip. "Well, pop me down a plughole!" exclaimed Trailer. "Look who it is, sir. It's old Oddsockz!"

6. "A million annoyances!" croaked the crown-prince, and he crowned his pal on the dome for the idea.

7. Shortly later, little Trailer was thinking of taking up flying—and Oddy was only too pleased to help him, with the aid of a special high-powered bomb!

8. There was a loud bang and Trailer skidded up into the sky. "See how he takes off!" cackled old Oddy. "I hope he vill not take on about it!"

9. Now it so happened that Maud and Maisie were having a spot of bother with their flying-bus. "Who will save us?" they cried. "I will!" warbled Trailer, stepping off the flying form.

10. In a tick or two Trailer had found out that it was the whatsername short-circuiting on the how-d'ye-do that was causing all the trouble, so he jolly soon put it right.

11. And that's how he became the hero of the camp, while Oddsockz and Serge snooped off, the beaten villains of the piece!

Laurie and Trailer; Chips; March 1940; (Albert Pease); © Amalgamated Press.

Sandy and Muddy; Knock-Out; April 1941; (Bill Radford); © Amalgamated Press.

SANDY and MUDDY — — — A KITTEN ON THE QUAY!

Herr Paul Pry; Magic; August 1940; (Artist Unknown); © D.C. Thomson.

HERR PAUL PRY

127

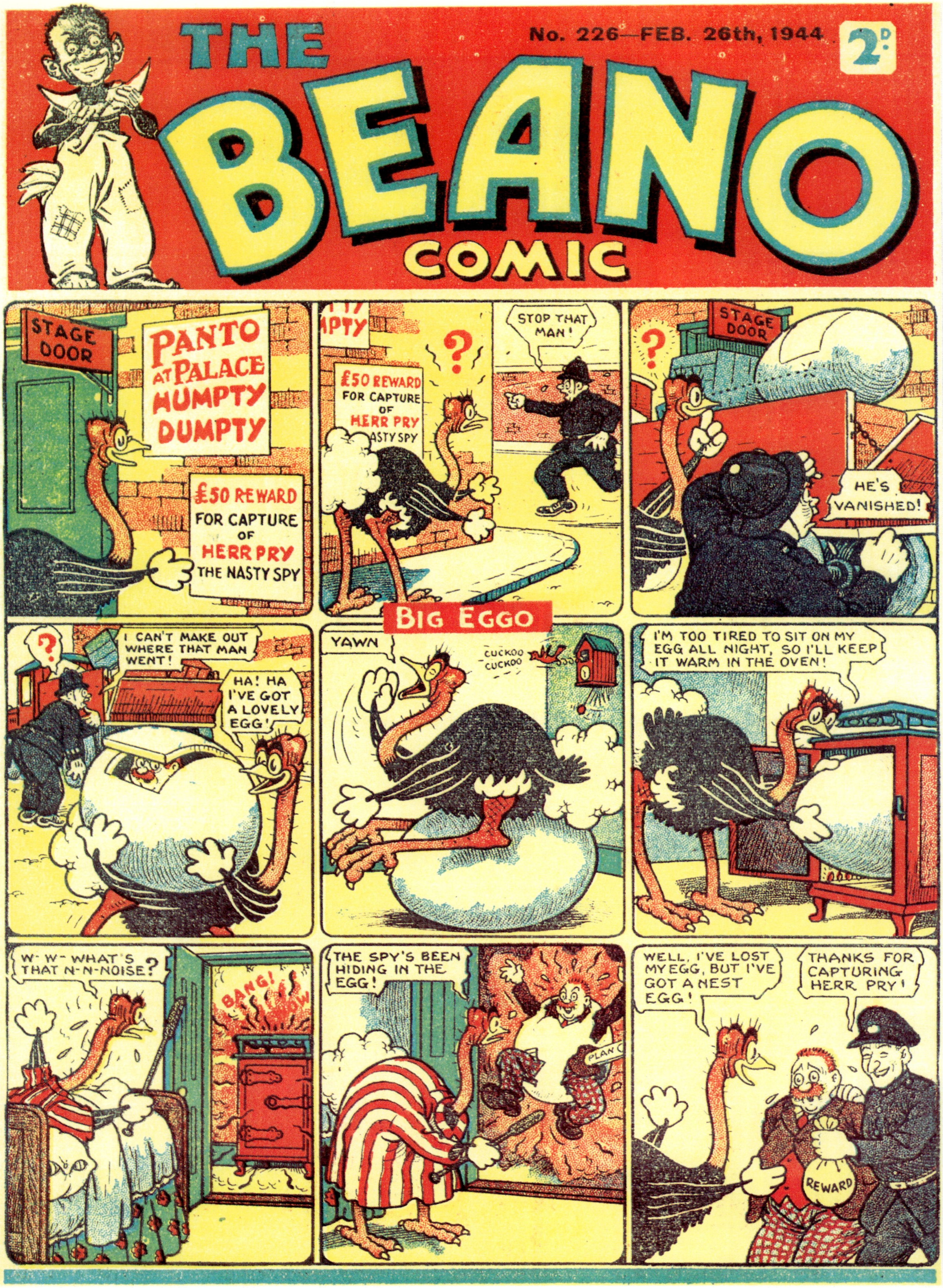

Big Eggo; Beano; February 1944; (Reg Carter); © D.C. Thomson.

Lord Snooty; Beano; March 1944; (Dudley Watkins); © D.C. Thomson.

WIRELESS WAR!

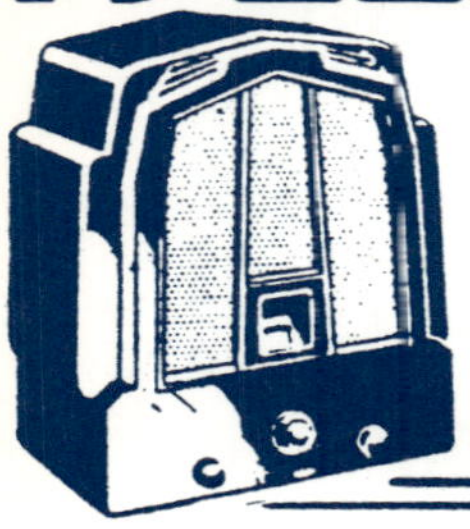

The wireless set as we called it, despite our favourite comic **Radio Fun**, was the main means of national communication during the war. It was also the main source of entertainment, even when 'Ateful Adolf beamed Lord Haw-Haw into our homes and shelters, courtesy of the old Radio Luxembourg transmitter. Haw-Haw soon brought ha-ha, thanks, naturally, to **Radio Fun**! Although artist John Jukes' visualisation of the traitor broadcaster is close to a caricature of a typical BBC newsreader, his first strip also makes reference to something many thought of as a stupid time-waster: the R.A.F. leaflet raids. In 1940 the BBC introduced early morning exercises to keep the nation fighting fit. Comics promptly latched on, thus keeping the nation's kids in fits! Even Hal Roach's Our Gang from Hollywood, now thoroughly naturalised by **The Dandy**, joined in.

Lord Haw-Haw; Radio Fun; April 1940; (John Jukes); © Amalgamated Press.

★ LORD HAW-HAW—The Broadcasting Humbug from Hamburg ★

Troddles; Jingles; September 1941; (Bertie Brown); © Amalgamated Press.

TRODDLES AND HIS PET TORTOISE... TONKY-TONK

LORD HAW-HAW—Broadcasting from Stations Ricebag and Humbug

Lord Haw-Haw; Radio Fun; March 1940; (John Jukes); © Amalgamated Press.

TOMMY HANDLEY
IT'S THAT MAN AGAIN, AND—FUNF!

Tommy Handley; Radio Fun; March 1940; (Reg Parlett); © Amalgamated Press.

131

CRACKERS

DO YOU WANT A THRILL? THEN YOU MUST READ "MEN OF THE SEA" ON PAGE TEN INSIDE!

2D

No. 581.] THE JOLLY ADVENTURES OF HAPPY HARRY AND HIS SISTER SUE. [April 6th, 1940.

1. DEAR ALL OF YOU,—Have you tried getting up early in the morning to do the wireless exercises? We all tried it—*once*! But only once!

2. Dad thought it would be a fine idea, and we listened to what the wireless told us to do. First, Dad opened the window.

3. It didn't tell him that his old shirt would come blowing in, and this rather spoiled his movements until we helped.

4. Sue and I soon pulled the shirt off him and then I thought I'd throw it out to Mum in the garden. "Catch, Mum!" I called, as I threw.

5. But the shirt never reached her, for just at that moment the window sash-line broke and down dropped the window!

6. "Oh dear!" I sighed. "We wanted Mum to catch the shirt, not the window! Still, we'll soon raise it!" But we didn't!

7. That window was jammed ever so tightly and at last Sue and I went outside to see if we could lift it easier from there!

8. We did, too! At our first try, up shot the window. "How's that, Dad?" I called. But he didn't answer at once.

9. As he fell back, he upset the wireless. He caught it, luckily, but he's not trying any more morning exercises. Cheers!—Yours, HARRY.

CRACKERS, THE PERKY PUP, IS WILD ABOUT THE WIRELESS!

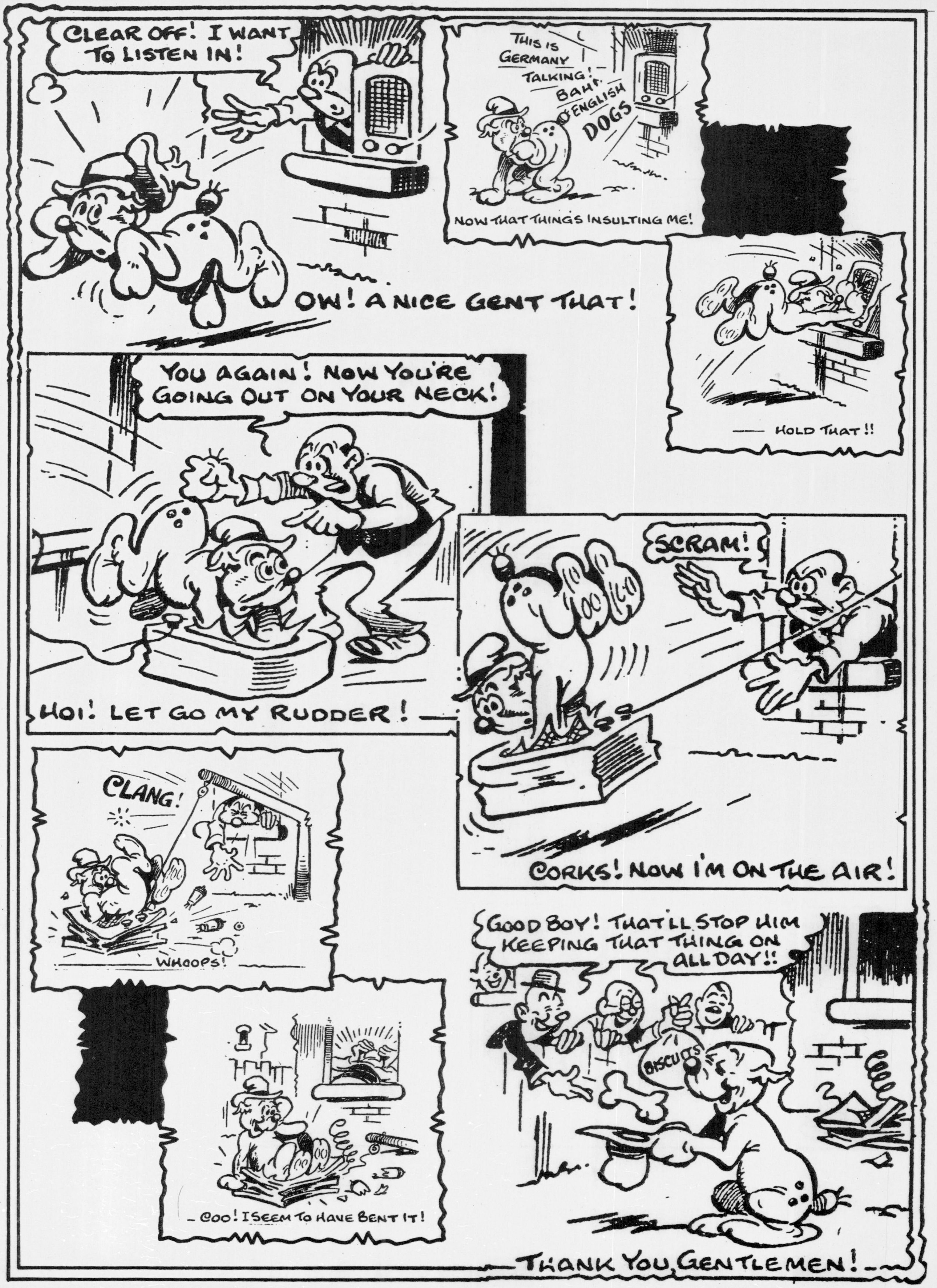

OUR GANG

All these boys and girls play in the famous Hal Roach films of "Our Gang," and appear here by courtesy of M-G-M.

Pete The Pup | Alfalfa Switzer | Scotty Beckett | Darla Hood | Billy Thomas | Porky Lee | Patsy May | Spanky McFarland | Buckwheat Thomas

1—The Gangsters are so lazy that if they had only to press a button to get anything they wanted, they would hire someone to press the button for them. And Spanky McFarland's even worse than the rest of the Gangsters. He's too lazy to get off a nettle, even if it's stinging him. So it just about gave him heart failure one lunch-time when his father said that there had been an announcement from the B.B.C. about some exercises that were to be on the wireless the next morning at seven-thirty, for Spanky's pa told him he'd have to get up and do them.

2—That afternoon you'd have thought, to see the Gangsters' gloomy faces, that all the sweet shops in town had closed down. All their fathers had decided to make them strong men. "We all have to get up to-morrow morning, too," said Alfalfa Switzer, when Spanky told him the sad news. "And I haven't done an exercise since that big stiff, Tug Kelly, poured a swarm of ants down my back. These wireless exercises are going to be awful," Scotty Beckett agreed. "I'll never have muscles anyway," he said. "We've got to get out of these exercises somehow."

3—Now somebody had given Alfalfa a toy microphone for his Christmas. If he fixed it to his wireless, he could stand and speak into it in the kitchen and his voice would come over the radio in the living-room, just as if he were broadcasting. So Scotty got the Gangsters to unfix all their wireless sets, then join them up again to Alfalfa's "mike." "And next morning, instead of the wireless exercises, you'll get a broadcast from Alfalfa!" exclaimed Scotty. "And then we'll be able to get back to bed."

4—Alfalfa took the "mike" to bed with him, ready to speak in to it the next morning, and everything went smoothly. At half-past seven, Spanky's father had rolled him out of bed, for that was the only way he could waken him. Then he got him all ready for his exercises. But they didn't get exercises. Instead they got an announcement that there would be no exercises that morning, and they were all to go back to bed. But they weren't to get off as easy as that, as they very soon found out.

5—Spanky's pa had an old army friend, Sergeant Tuff, who held drill classes in the town. "Since there's no drill on the wireless, you're going to get drill from him, Spanky, my lad," pa boomed. "And your friends will be going there, too. I'll fix it with their parents." So the Gangsters found themselves in Sergeant Tuff's gym that morning doing all sorts of exercises.

6—"Gosh!" said Buckwheat. "I've thrown my chest out so much it feels like it's gone away altogether." But Sergeant Tuff gave the Gangster's more than physical jerks, for next he made them jump over horses and other things. The Gangsters had never been so fed-up in their lives. "An hour of this is just sixty minutes too long!" groaned Spanky.

Our Gang; Dandy; January 1940; (Dudley Watkins); © D.C. Thomson.

7—By the time the first lesson was finished, the Gangsters looked as if they'd just had a stand-up fight with a British tank regiment. "Gee!" moaned Billy Thomas. "My backbone's shifted round to the front with me bending down so often!" Still, Sergeant Tuff wasn't contented. "I'll expect you back to-morrow!" he barked. "And if you're not any better, I'll lick the stuffing out of you." When Our Gang heard this, their faces became so long they just about tripped over them as they limped away. They were so tired after their exercises it took them four hours to do a normal ten-minutes' walk to the Gang Hut. But when they got there, they got an idea to escape Sergeant Tuff.

8—They decided to get all the balloons in town they could lay their hands on and stuff them under their jerseys to make it look as if they had developed huge chests from doing the keep-fit exercises. What a job they had collecting these balloons! First of all they had to get all the jam jars they could find. Porky was about sick because he had to finish off the jam in ten of them before he got the jars. Then they chased after all the junk-men they could see to swop the jars for balloons. After that they blew up so many balloons they were out of breath for a couple of weeks. "It won't be only our chests that will be bigger," said Scotty. "Our cheeks are blown out, now."

9—Anyway, they were soon all rigged out with bulges all over them. "Crikey!" said Alfalfa. "We're like a strong men's outing." They certainly looked young giants. Scotty Beckett looked queer at first, though, for the balloons had all slipped to one side. But Spanky soon pointed it out to him. "Look, Scotty," he said. "You're only half a strong man. You look as if you'd had a correspondence course in keep-fit and lost half of the lessons in the post." After that, the Gangsters went home.

10—Spanky's mother was in the kitchen when he went in, but she left his food out for him. When she came in from the kitchen and saw him sitting there like a young Samson, she just about phoned for the ambulance. She thought she'd put too much self-raising powder in the pudding and blown him up. But she got a worse shock when Spanky ate three times as much dinner as usual. He explained it was Sergeant Tuff's course that had made him that way, and that he was going to grow even bigger.

11—The plan worked. Spanky wasn't allowed back to Sergeant Tuff's class. And it was the same with the other Gangsters, who weren't to be allowed to the class either. So all the Gangsters got a holiday from the class that afternoon, and only Porky wasn't pleased at the way their dodge had worked. When he walked in, his ma didn't recognise him, and threw him out.

12—All went well till the Gangsters were walking along a wall trying a trick Sergeant Tuff had taught them. The balloons helped them to keep their balance, but suddenly Buckwheat's balloon slipped out of place and he toppled into a tar barrel. Gosh, when he came out of the tar barrel he was the best blacked-out thing in town! So he had to go home for a bath.

13—Then things came out in more ways than one. For when Buckwheat got ready for his bath his mother discovered the balloon under his jersey. The Gangsters, who were waiting anxiously at the door of Buckwheat's house, saw this and went pale. "Golly!" said Alfalfa. "Mrs Thomas will tell our fathers and mothers and I'll get the biggest licking since the doctor told dad to take more exercise." So the Gangsters began to head for the next town at about sixty miles an hour.

14—But they had to come back for tea, and then they didn't only get a licking. That wouldn't have been so bad. But they were all sent back to Sergeant Tuff's till the end of the week with a note to make them go harder at it than ever. And Sergeant Tuff certainly obeyed the letter. He marched the Gangsters and drilled them so much they would have found hard labour in a prison like a rest cure. "There's one thing, though," sighed Porky Lee. "We'll be able to run away from the cops better now!"

TO BLAZES WITH THE FIREMEN!

To fight the fires we had the N.F.S. and the A.F.S., the National Fire Service and the Auxiliary Fire Service – plus the Casey Court version, the Nashunal Fire Servise, fire cheef B. Baggs, Esq. The A.F.S. was well represented by Volunteer Fireman Stan, whom Lionel Grumblin interviewed in **Radio Fun's** 'In Town This Week,' courtesy of the great George Parlett (known, by the by, as 'Froth' to his pals. We wonder why?). Eric Roberts' pioneering Podge was a family sit-com strip that ran in red-and-blue on the back page of **The Dandy.** If you have seen the brilliant film, **Hope and Glory,** you may wonder if its writer/director might not have read this very strip when he was a boy in the war.

Podge; Dandy; December 1940; (Eric Roberts); © D.C. Thomson.

Casey Court; Chips; March 1942; (Albert Pease); © Amalgamated Press.

Pansy Potter; Beano; October 1943; (Basil Blackaller); © D.C. Thomson.

IN TOWN THIS WEEK!

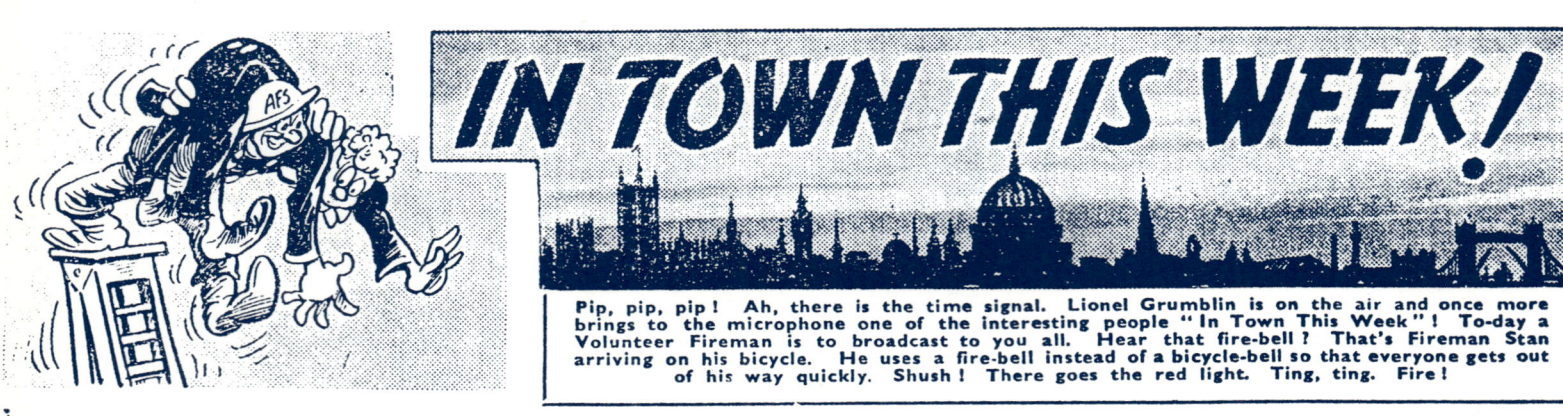

Pip, pip, pip! Ah, there is the time signal. Lionel Grumblin is on the air and once more brings to the microphone one of the interesting people "In Town This Week"! To-day a Volunteer Fireman is to broadcast to you all. Hear that fire-bell? That's Fireman Stan arriving on his bicycle. He uses a fire-bell instead of a bicycle-bell so that everyone gets out of his way quickly. Shush! There goes the red light. Ting, ting. Fire!

"Hallo, listeners-in, are you comfy? Grab a cosy armchair if you can — help yourself to some nice bread and dripping while I fetch Volunteer Fireman Stan.

Now Stan isn't always a fireman, in the daytime he taps a typewriter —

A clerk said to me at the office, 'Hi, Stan — switch the fire on, old scout!' I said (feeling vexed), 'Light a fire? — Tut! — What next? I don't light fires, I just put 'em out!'

The big noise down at our fire station was an officer named Captain Sozzle a hard drinker he, swigging pints of cold tea, sucking same from the pot through a nozzle!

Ah, here he comes in with his choppah, the door now resembles firewood, (he did not use the handle, that would be quite a scandal, and he chops while the chopping is good).

— When the old office closes he grabs tin hat and hoses to start work as a part-time firefighter!

They gave me a small fire to start with, they burned some brown paper and fat, — it smelt like that cigar you're smoking, but I quickly altered all that!

Will you please tell us all why you joined it? Did you envy the real firemen bold? Carry on, Fireman Stan!"

"Well, it's like this, old man, I enjoy fires 'cos I can't stand the cold!

I sleep with my uniform handy, my axe to my belt I can buckle, when the fire alarm goesies, from boots I tip roses, while from tinhat I pluck honeysuckle!

In Town This Week; Radio Fun; September 1939; (George Parlett); © Amalgamated Press.

UP A FIRE ESCAPE THEY SENT ME CLIMBING — CAPTAIN SOZZLE SAID "YOU CAN GO HIGHER!" — BUT THE TOP RUNG WAS CHARRED AND MY BRACES I JARRED, AFTER WHICH I SAID "SOZ — YOU'RE A FIBBER!"

MY JOB AT A FIRE IS IMPORTANT BUT I GET WET FROM TOPKNOT TO TOES — I HAVE TO STICK FINGERS IN PUNCTURES, OR SIT ON LARGE LEAKS IN THE HOSE!

A NATIONAL SERVICE INSPECTION — A MARCH PAST IN COLUMNS OF THREE — HERE'S A PRESS PHOTOGRAPH OF OUR SECTION — (THE MAN IN STEP IS, OF COURSE, ME!)

"EYES RIGHT!"

WHEN I SEE A FLAME I GET BUSY — AND OUT GOES EACH BLAZE THAT I MEET — I BLOW OUT PEOPLE'S MATCHES OR CANDLES, AND NIGHTWATCHMEN'S FIRES IN THE STREET!

"HO! ME LAST MATCH!!"

ON RESERVE AT THE STATION ONE EVENING I SIGHED FOR A REAL FIRE TO FIGHT. WELL, MY WISH I SOON GOT AND IT WASN'T HALF HOT, 'COS THE FIRE STATION BLAZED UP QUITE BRIGHT!

THE BRIGADE HAD GONE OUT FOR A BEANO, THEY'D LEFT ME IN CHARGE OF THE SHACK, SO I JUST KEPT THE FIRE NICELY GOING, UNTIL FIRE BRIGADE COULD COME BACK!

THE CAPTAIN WAS JUST A BIT SHIRTY — HE SAID TO ME 'STAN, AFTER THAT — YOU CAN JUST LEAVE FIRES BE IF YOU'D LIKE TO PLEASE ME YOU CAN PUT OUT THE FIRE STATION CAT!'

"LIONEL GRUMBLIN NOW THANKS FIREMAN STANLEY — FOR A STORY LIKE HIS WE'VE BEEN YEARNING! BY THE WAY, WHAT'S THAT SMELL? CAN YOU SNIFF IT AS WELL? IS IT SOMETHING AFIRE OR JUST BURNING?"

FIREMAN STAN MUST NOW BUZZ OFF AND LEAVE US — TO A FIRE HE MUST GIVE HIS ATTENTION — WHEN THE 'CONFLAG HE DOUSES, HE'LL NEED SOME NEW 'TROUSIS' 'COS THEY'RE SINGED IN A PLACE I DAREN'T MENTION!"

"FIRE!"

NEXT WEEK'S INTERVIEW WILLIE BOUNCE OF THE BALLOON BARRAGE

Casey Court; Chips; February 1941; (Albert Pease); © Amalgamated Press

LUVLY GRUB!

FUN ON THE RATION

The food shortage meant no fun shortage in the comics. The official order was 'Dig for Victory!', translated by the Casey Court Kids as 'Grow Your Own Grub!' They set to with a will, and a shovel, filling watering-cans with vinegar so the onions would come up pickled! Peter Piper, who was always Picking People Out of Pickles of a different kind, tootled his magic flute to bring the famous Dig for Victory poster to life, while Tiger Tim and the Bruin Boys tried to grow a jam tart tree! Our Ernie of **The Knockout** met a fat lad from the P.T.E.T.C., a corps we'd all like to have joined: the Peace Time Eats Ttraining Corps! But it wasn't only food that was rationed. Clothes were, too, and Casey Court had an answer for that one, a Clothes Wivout Coupons Week.

The Bruin Boys; Tiger Tim's Weekly; February 1940; (Artist Unknown); © Amalgamated Press.

141

PETER PIPER
PICKING PEOPLE OUT OF PICKLES

"Gosh! Look at that!" hear Peter say.
"That cart-horse has just run away!"
But ePter Piper's mighty slick,
So now he blows his pipes real quick.

He plays his pipes now with a sigh
To a big, tough cowboy guy
Who's on a poster that is near.
He'll stop that horse now, never fear!

All the spectators get a treat.
That cowboy's dashed o'er the street.
Then, cool as ice and without a cheep,
On to that nag's back see him leap.

Now when that nag's brought to a halt,
Pete's thanked by the owner of the colt.
But o'er a dame's lawn it has run,
So on his pipes Pete blows like fun.

He charms a poster, as you see,
Which tells you, "DIG FOR VICTORY."
Upon it there are men with picks,
Just watch them now—they're full of tricks.

The foreman shouts to them, "Come on!
We're going to fix this lady's lawn."
And fix that garden, they sure do,
In fact, it soon looks good as new.

But now hear that old lady croakin'
"Oh, dearie me! My fence is broken."
When Peter sees it, his blood curdles,
So he pipes a lad who's jumping hurdles.

That hurdler though is far from dense,
And soon he's fixed that lady's fence.
He fits the bundle o'er the crack,
Then to his poster he goes back.

The lady thanks Pete with a smile
Because he worked in such fine style.
She says, "Oh, Pete, you were so willing."
And gives our lad a big bright shilling!

Peter Piper, Magic; August 1940; (Dudley Watkins); © D.C. Thomson.

142

Cried lad, " I know Air Training Corps,
And ' A.T.S.' and a whole lot more,
But what is ' P.T.E.T.C.' ?
By gum, that's a new one on me ! "

While lad were wondering and in doubt
What these initals were about.
Fat lad who wore them, murmured " Ee,
Big orange is the stuff for me ! "

Cried Ernie, " By gum ! Man alive,
He doesn't look like ' under five.'
What ever next will feller do ?
Ee, my—he's got bananas, too ! "

He gave banana to our lad,
But that weren't all the fat chap had,
Would you believe he'd toffees, too ?
Well, that he had—as true as true !

Cried he to Ernie. " Coo, I'm glad
I met you, 'cos I like you, lad,
So come with me to our H.Q.
And I'll show you what our Corps do."

Said lad, " By gum, this is the stuff.
I'll join your Corps if I'm old enough.
Cried fat lad, " You'll like it you will.
Here's choc bars, lad. Just eat your fill ! "

Snack bar were next place Ernie saw,
Where grub was stacked from roof to floor ;
Butter, eggs, ice-cream, and ham,
Jelly, tarts, and strawberry jam.

Fat chap took bread and spread upon it,
A pound of butter, and then on it
Dumped strawberry jam, heavy and thick
And yelled " G'wan, lad ! Eat it, quick !

" Then try some jelly and cream. Don't stop.
'Cos next we come to ginger pop,
And then there's lots of fruity cake :
Come, eat up, lad, for goodness' sake !

Cried Ernie, " Ee, I like your Corps,
I wish I'd know'd of it before,
By gum, these chocs are very nice,
And I've got my eye on a creamy ice ! "

Said fat lad, " You must join us, chummy,
And get some real eats in your tummy,
Though, mind, our training's pretty tough,
'Cos we have to eat more when we've had enough.

Cried lad, " O my ! You're telling me :
I don't think I shall want my tea,
I'd like to lie quite still, I would,
This peace-time feeling's not so good ! "

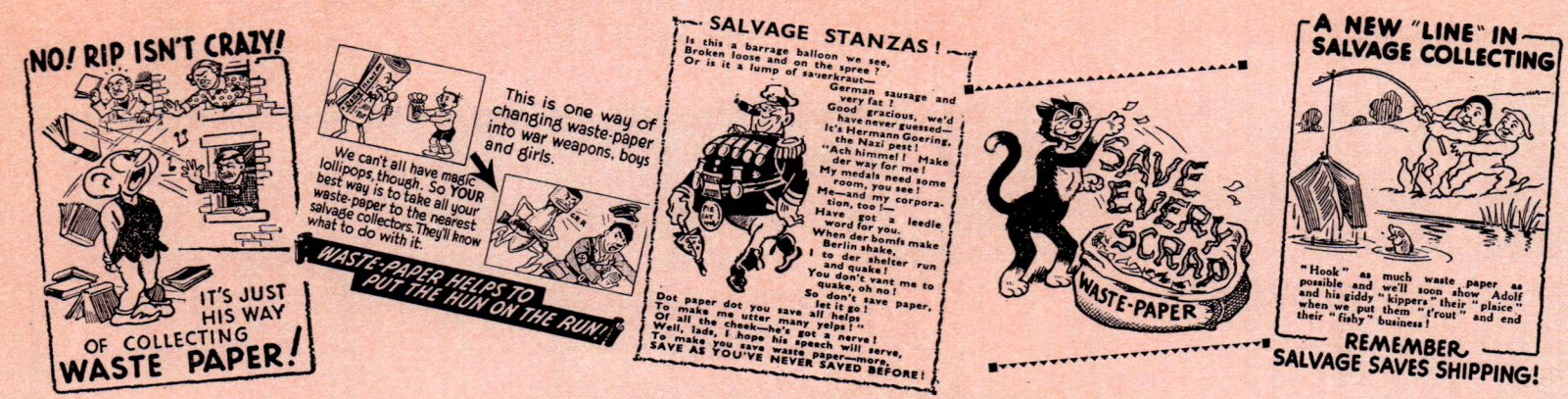

SALVAGE!
THE CHAPS FOR A SCRAP!

It wasn't only our lads in khaki and two shades of blue who were good for a scrap. Here on the Home Front the comics did their share, plugging paper salvage, scrap metal drives, and all the other ways youngsters could lend the proverbial hand. Comics regularly featured favourite funsters bidding their readers to chuck their old comics onto the salvage stacks and Help Hitler Where It Hurts. We did our duty then, and now we wish we hadn't – especially when we see the peacetime prices asked for old wartime comics! How Addy and Hermy and Musso the Wop must be laughing now – between jabs of the pitchfork, of course. Something else we could do was to Save and Stop the Squander Bug. As long as we saved tuppence for our favourite comic, of course. One thing we were allowed to keep was – secrets!

RONNIE ROY . . . . . . THE INDIARUBBER BOY

SOOTY SNOWBALL

Young Sooty Snowball's come to stay
From desert lands far, far away.
He's really cute, this funny japer—
And now he's out to get waste-paper.

He scampers off home for his cart,
Then he looks for a place to start.
He can't find paper scraps and so
In the library see him go.

The bloke in charge is fast asleep
As through the doorway see Soot creep
And grab the books off the shelves. Wow!
Soot's sure got plenty paper now!

On to his cart he piles the tomes,
Then off around the streets he roams,
His mind with bright ideas fills
When he sees a guy who's sticking bills

He thinks, "There's lots of paper there!"
And so the cute nig starts to tear
The posters all down off the wall—
If that guy spots him he'll sure bawl!

Soot piles the posters on his cart,
Then down the street he must depart.
The bill-sticker sure thinks it's weird
That all his bills have disappeared.

As past a bank young Sooty's going
He spots a bloke who's busy stowing
Paper scraps into a case.
A cute smile spreads o'er Sooty's face.

The bloke's back's turned to light his pipe
And Soot thinks the time is ripe
To add the bag to his collection.
We sure hope he escapes detection!

But Sooty's done it! He's sure smart—
He's put the bag now on his cart,
He's got as much as he can take,
So for the depot see him make.

The depot's where the stuff's all brought,
And into it comes our black tot.
"Here's plenty paper," hear him yell,
And all the folks think Sooty's swell.

But they don't think so in a minute,
The bag is opened, and gosh! In it
There's lots of banknotes! Soot looks blank—
Those guys think he has robbed a bank!

The man from whom Soot pinched that bag
Was a burglar—that case held his swag!
The cops soon clear young Sooty, though,
And reward him with a bag of dough!

Sooty Snowball: Magic: August 1940: (Bob MacGillivray) © D.C. Thomson.

COMICAL CAMOUFLAGE!

Desperate Dan; Dandy; February 1942; (Dudley Watkins); © D.C. Thomson.

A PENNY A DAY KEEPS OLD HITLER AWAY!

Our Ernie; Knock-Out; June 1943; (A.J. Kelly); © Amalgamated Press.

OUR ERNIE
MRS. ENTWHISTLE'S LITTLE LAD.

No doubt you've seen the Squander Bug—
Chap with long ears and ugly mug,
Who will pretend to be your friend
If he thinks you've got cash to spend.

Cried Squander Bug to Ernie, "Ee,
You've got a money-box, I see;
Come on, lad, let's go blue some dough—
It doesn't matter how, you know!"

So they bought rezin at a store,
And then lad asked what stuff were for,
And shopman said "'Tis used to twiddle
The 'Hi-diddle-diddle' out of a fiddle."

So lad must needs buy fiddle, too,
And Squander Bug then said he knew,
Posh music shop, where lad could go,
And spend a whole great wad of dough.

Cried Squander Bug, "Keep spending, lad.
You're the best customer I've had;
I like your posh new bob-tailed coat;
Now buy a car, you silly goat!"

Cried Ernie, "Ee, I've had a spree!
I think I'll buzz off home for tea!"
Said Squander Bug, "Nay, that won't do!
Hotel de Ritz is place for you!"

So off they went to posh hotel,
Where everything were swish and swell,
And you could fill your tummy tight,
With grub at thirty-bob a bite.

Head waiter said, "Vot vill you chew?"
And handed lad the "Me-and-you!"
Cried Squander Bug, "Bring all you can!
We want to waste it, my good man!"

The waiter brought the bill for tea.
(It measured nearly two foot three);
But Ernie found, to his dismay.
He'd nothing left with which to pay.

Result were lad were flung from place,
And as street pavement met his face,
The Squander Bug cried, "Good-bye, kid!
I enjoyed that squandering, I did!"

'Twere lucky for our lad that he
Were only dreaming, as you see;
When he thought street had hit his head,
'Twas 'cos he'd fallen out of bed.

His money-box still held his dough,
So when Sis said, "Ee, lad, y'know,
Some Savings Stamps is things for thee!"
Lad cried, "You bet! You're telling me!"

148

INFORMATION ON RATION !

Casey Court; Chips; October 1941; (Cyril Price); © Amalgamated Press.

WORKERS PLAYTIME !

Tin Can Tommy; Beano; November 1943; (George Drysdale); © D.C. Thomson.

149

PUTTING THE TIN HAT ON IT!

Podge; Dandy; November 1940; (Eric Roberts); © D.C. Thomson.

SHUSH! IT'S A SECRET!

Calling all Chipites on an awfully secret wavelength for this week only. By kind permission of the Ministry of Super Secrets we are able to get the kids of Casey Court to reveal you some of the very hush-hush War Secrets, so close your eyes, stuff your fingers in your ears and promise not to tell more than a thousand people all you get to know. Aha! What's all that? It is young Arbuthnot Oylcan, who has sneaked in disguised as someone else by the simple method of washing his face, and we observe that he has brought with him a design for a smoke-screen. And what does Billy Baggs think about it? He's in a bit of a fog at the moment, but he'll see through it!

Casey Court; Chips; November 1940; (Albert Pease); © Amalgamated Press.

Lord Snooty; Beano; October 1943; (Dudley Watkins); © D.C. Thomson.

ALLIES:

FROM DOWN UNDER AND OVER THERE!

In on the action from the outset was, of course, the British Empire, and it was not long before a fair dinkum specimen of an Aussie Anzac left Matilda waltzing around the billabongs and came up from Down Under to breeze onto the front page of **Radio Fun** with a hearty handout of gaspers to Big-Hearted Arthur and Stinker Murdoch. Those were the days when cigarette smoking was an international hobby: today even a dog-end is censored in the comics! From over there to over here, the Yanks were coming, and sure enough one G.I. turned up, jeep and all, in **The Knockout.** Note also that this **Deed-a-Day Danny** escapade introduces that forgotten military vehicle, the D.U.K.W., called colloquially, the Duck.

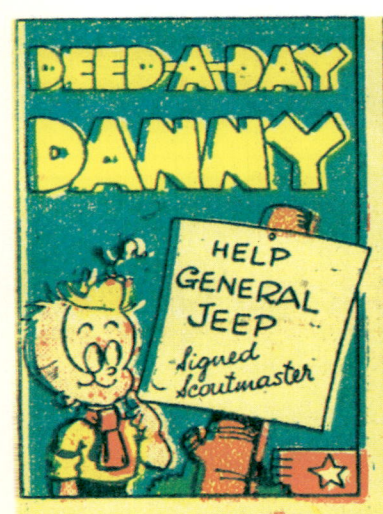

153

V FOR VICTORY!

Victory was in the air the night they let the lights go on in London, just like the popular song had promised. The Casey Court Light Brigade charged across the back page of **Chips** in true topical celebration. Then, at long last, came Victory, not just once but twice – two of them, to match the number of fingers we had been sticking up for six years. V.E. (Victory in Europe) Day in 1945 is reflected in the colourful covers of **Chips** and **Mickey Mouse,** while we illustrate V.J. (Victory in Japan) Day in 1946 with those twin shafts of show business, **Radio Fun** and **Film Fun.**

Weary Willie and Tired Tim; Chips; August 1945; (Percy Cocking); © Amalgamated Press.

Mickey Mouse © Walt Disney Company; Mickey Mouse Weekly; June 1945; (Victor Ibbetson); © Odhams Press.

Tommy Handley; Radio Fun; June 1946; (Bertie Brown); © Amalgamated Press.

FIRST IN THE FUN PARADE!

GRAND VICTORY HOLIDAY NUMBER — Film Fun — 3d
SOMETHING TO CHEER ABOUT — AN ALL STAR SHOW

No. 1,377.   Every Tuesday.   June 8th, 1946.

LAUREL & HARDY

Our Couple of "Wags" Will See That Your Spirits Don't "Flag" During The Holiday!

This Week: "L. AND H. TAKE A FRONT SEAT!"

Panel 1 (Olly to Stan in deck-chair): "May I remind you, Stanley, that it is Victory Holiday to-day and WE ARE GOING TO THE PROCESSION. Put that book away and get ready." — "I'll be ready in a jiffy, Olly." *(Stan reading "Professor Poppit's Guide to the Weather")*

Hallo, Folks. It was a beautiful day, and Olly was looking forward to seeing the Victory procession. When he peeped out into the garden to see what Stan was doing he saw him reclining in a deck-chair. Olly told Stan to get ready.

Panel 2: "Great pip! Stan! Why are you dressed up like that on a beautiful day like to-day?" — "Professor Poppit states that plenty of clothes keep the cold out, so I thought that all these togs would keep the heat out!"

2. When Olly came out half an hour later he found Stan wearing a thick overcoat, a muffler and balaclava helmet. Not exactly the right type of clothing to wear on a hot day! It wasn't surprising Olly wanted to know exactly why little Stan had all those togs on.

Panel 3: "I can't take you out to the Victory procession like that. Go in and put on something suitable for the hot weather." — "Okay, Olly, you are always right!"

3. It was then that our little lump of laughter explained that he had read in his book that plenty of clothes kept the cold out. He thought if he put on plenty of clothes they would keep the heat out. Olly told Stan to put on something suitable for the warm weather.

Panel 4: "I must admit you were right. I feel much cooler in this suitable clothing, Olly." — "We'll never get a good view of the procession if you don't hurry! You see how I am dressed? Well, go in and put on similar clothing!"

4. Just look at Stan, folks. As if he could go out into the crowd and view the procession dressed in a bathing suit! I can understand Olly getting a bit aggranoyed with Stanley. Our mass of merriment told Stan to go in and put on similar clothing to his own.

Panel 5: "How's this, Olly?" — "You're the giddy limit Stan! I don't know why I don't take a running jump at you and spafflicate your wishbone!"

5. Of course, Olly meant that he wanted Stan to put on some of his own clothes which were similar to those he was wearing himself. As usual, Stan got hold of the wrong end of the stick, and put on some of Olly's clothing, which was too big. Poor old Stan!

Panel 6: "How go back indoors again and put on YOUR white shirt and grey flannels!" — "I really wish you would make up your mind, Olly."

6. Olly went off the deep end like a giant rocket. I really think that Stan does try Olly's patience a little too much. Olly shouted to Stan to come inside and put on a white shirt and grey flannels. Now, folks, I think that's an order little Stanley should be capable of carrying out quite correctly. Please step into the next picture.

Panel 7: "I could not find my white shirt and grey flannels, Olly, so I put on my night-shirt made of RED flannel." — "What a prize dope if ever there was one!"

7. He's not done it again! Listen to him explaining to Olly that as he couldn't get a white shirt and grey flannels, he's put on his night-shirt made of red flannel. I mean to say. I can understand Olly getting a bit annoyed with Stan, and at times wanting to slap him smartly and severely on the left wrist. *(Continued on page 16.)*

158

8. And so Olly decided to dress Stan himself. Grasping him by the right hand, he dashed into the house, realising that if something wasn't done and done quickly, neither of them would see the procession. Let's hope everything will be okey-doke now. I've a feeling that if anything else goes wrong now, they'll miss the show.

9. Here you may observe our lucky lads arriving, properly dressed and certainly looking the part. However, there was a terrific crowd, and it looked as if neither of the boys would be able to get much view of the procession. Yes, I'm afraid Stan and Olly will have to take a back seat on this occassion, which is really rather a pity, eh?

10. It was quite plain to Olly that they wouldn't get as much as a glimpse of the passing show. He proceeded to tick Stan off from a great height for taking such a long time to get ready. Our little lump of laughter said it was a shame he was blamed for everything that went wrong. But just you wait a minute, dear readers!

11. Then a strange thing happened. A little bloke who had been pushing and shoving to get through the crowd suddenly collapsed in a faint, and a couple of first-aid blokes dashed forward to do their stuff. They shouted to all and sundry that the fellow wanted air, and that he must be taken right to the front away from the crowd.

12. It only happens once in about every five years that little Stanley thinks of a good idea, but I really must say that I think he deserves full marks for this notion, plus a couple of hearty pats on the back. Stan suggested to Olly that they should pretend to faint in the hope that they would also be taken to the front of the mob.

13. They quite thought the first-aid men would take them to the front of the crowd, but, unfortunately, the ambulance boys came to the decision that Stan and Olly looked like a couple of hospital cases, so they were yanked along to the hospital in the jolly old van. It looks as if once again Stan has got Olly into yet another fine mess.

14. Strange to relate, everything turned out okey-doke and just as the doctor ordered. The jolly old doc, having run the rule over Stan and Olly, came to the conclusion there was nothing wrong with them. He had heard they had fainted in the crowd, and he said it was due to the excitement and all that. He was a jolly old sport, was the doc. He asked our couple of cough-drops if they would agree to view the procession from the hospital window, as it was due to pass in a couple of shakes. And did the boys accept the offer? I should think they did. Little Stanley's idea turned out okay, after all, and they proceeded straightaway to take a couple of front seats.

15. And so our lucky lads were able to view the procession, as you may observe. Their cheers were loud and long, and they thoroughly enjoyed the show. By the way, they have asked me to tell you that they hope you will enjoy your Victory Holiday as much as they did. And I wish you all the best, too. L. and H. will be present and correct once again next week, in their latest adventure entitled: "Ringing the Changes!" All the best and brightest to one and all until next Toosday when Stan and Olly shine again.—Yours merrily,

Eddie, The Happy Editor

PASS THIS COPY TO A CHUM AND YOU WILL OBLIGE YOUR OLD FRIEND—EDDIE, THE HAPPY EDITOR.

Laurel and Hardy; Film Fun; June 1946; (Freddie Crompton); © Amalgamated Press.

It was all over bar the shouting, and there was a whole lot of shouting to be done! It would be a long time before British comics could overcome the loss of size due to paper rationing, the loss of colour due to ink shortage, and the loss of many of their best artists and writers in action. The comic characters recovered quickest of all, of course: no long waits for demob papers for them. Private Billy Muggins and Mousey of **The Wonder's** page one soon turned in their tin titfers for civvy suits and signed on in the building trade. Unfortunately their old sergeant did likewise and turned up as their furious foreman! But that's another story, as they say. Let us stay within those wartorn years and close with Charlie Chucklechops' prediction of what to do with your old wartime souvenirs.

PEACE PUDD'N!

Charlie Chucklechops; Jingles; December 1944; (Albert Peasel; © Amalgamated Press.